CW00822491

SOFT SKILLS
—*for*—
HARD PEOPLE

A Practical Guide to Emotional Intelligence
for Rational Leaders

HELENA KIM, PHD

Copyright © 2020 by Helena Kim, PhD.

All rights reserved. This book or any portion thereof may not be reproduced or used in any manner whatsoever without the express written permission of the publisher except for the use of brief quotations in a book review.

Publishing Services provided by Paper Raven Books
Printed in the United States of America
First Printing, 2020

Paperback ISBN: 978-1-8381998-0-7
Hardback ISBN: 978-1-8381998-1-4

To my husband, Sanjay Sinha,
my greatest teacher and life's gift.

TABLE OF CONTENTS

INTRODUCTION

In my 25 years of coaching and training leaders, teams, and graduate students, I have time and time again run into the same obstacle: The "soft skills" so often promoted in leadership books and coaching models simply don't work for many rational and pragmatic people. These types of skills tend to be too emotionally laden, too obscure, or just not practical in the face of fast-paced, demanding day-to-day operations.

While we can all agree that the old-fashioned "get over it and get on with it" approach is outdated and ineffective as a leadership model, the pendulum seems to have swung too far the other direction. Now, coaching and leadership are defined by vague feelings-based language, the need for empathy on tap, or the foregoing of results for the pursuit of well-being and vulnerability. We've traded boxing gloves for kid gloves, and frankly, neither one works on its own.

If you're like me, you've probably asked yourself whether it's possible that we've gone too far into the heart and, in the process, lost touch with the head. The happy medium resides somewhere *between* heart and head, where you'll find such psychological states as trust, curiosity, and courage. With these qualities, you'll be able to roll up your proverbial sleeves to skillfully manage conflict, complaints, and tough conversations and fulfil the motivational needs for your team to be happy and successful.

This book offers a different way for leaders across diverse industries and sectors to understand and practice people skills. The emphasis is more on "doing" rather than just "being" emotionally intelligent. You'll find principles based on values that *make sense* rather than *feel good*.

I'D LIKE TO INVITE YOU TO READ THIS BOOK IF...

You are a leader who is already applying leadership or coaching principles in your role, but something just isn't quite jiving for you. Maybe it's coming to practical grips with seemingly broad concepts such as self-awareness, empathy, or active listening.

You are a pragmatist who can't help but roll your eyes at the elusive or emotion-based ideas found in some of the leadership training models. Do you cringe when you're asked to open your heart, be vulnerable, and develop more empathy? This book is especially for leaders who may be a bit cynical or apprehensive about conventional emotional wisdom that feels fuzzy or vague.

You want your team to be successful. Your team wants the same, and the prerequisite is that they are inspired and motivated. This comes naturally if they're competent, valued, and growing. You have the power to fulfil these motivational needs by applying rational soft skills.

You're a newbie at coaching and leading or aspire to a leadership role. This book serves as a template for skills that will help you handle difficult interpersonal situations more effectively. This is not an academic book with citations and references. It's a simple guide to take with you as you move up in your career.

In all my years of working in psychology, education, and executive coaching, I've studied many models looking for principles to apply in service to my students and clients. Some of what I found has been useful; some, not so much. In my efforts to simplify things for myself, I've distilled hundreds of concepts and insights and made note of what works, what doesn't, and why. Over time, I realized I was developing my own working model, which challenges conventional wisdom about being emotionally intelligent in coaching and leadership. I'm a fan of emotional intelligence, but a bigger fan of actually "doing" emotional intelligence.

I'm happy to share these tried-and-tested insights and interventions, which may be game changers in coaching leadership, especially for people who, like me, lean on the side of being "hard" (cerebral realists, cynics, pragmatists) yet are open to applying soft skills for the sake of their team and their performance. This book will resonate for fellow "hard people," who commune with their proverbial grumpy old grouch within, and leaders who are a bit pessimistic or feel burdened by all these supposed soft skills. In academia, we were taught to be critical of fluffy pop psychology and to some, soft skills development may feel similarly fuzzy. I was one of the skeptical academics. However, as social scientists, business school professors, and neuroscientists began demonstrating the positive correlation between leaders' emotional intelligence and employees' success, satisfaction, and productivity (not to mention higher evaluation ratings for the leaders), I was forced to reconsider my skepticism. At the same time, I also discovered that it takes a bit more tangibility for us hard people to be happy, optimistic, and convinced of the value of soft skills. This book is a quick toolkit for my hardened readers who need a rational take on emotional intelligence so they can lead without necessarily converting to the warm and fuzzy.

WHAT'S INSIDE?

What you hold in your hands is my unique, slightly edgy, and irreverent take on the conventional tropes used in coaching and leadership development. The words will be familiar: conflict, self-awareness, empathy, active listening, and so on. But my take on them will be distinctive and might even feel a bit jarring. Stick with me. My goal is to quickly and effectively shift your perspective on coaching and leadership skills by sharing my distillations into a handful of easily digestible and doable insights and practices.

TERMINOLOGY

There is a huge overlap between emotional intelligence, coaching, and leadership, so let's bring them together under the heading of **"coaching leadership"** for the purpose of this book.

Coaching is not new and continues to be a pervasive part of leadership principles and training in the 21st century. It originated as an elegantly recycled form of counseling psychology, specifically solution-focused brief therapy, which is an offshoot of cognitive behavioral therapy. In cognitive behavioral therapy, the work generally revolves around the present and the future, using strengths you already have or creating new tools to move forward and keep moving forward.

Today, most successful team leaders have undergone coaching training. Consultants like me are hired to coach and train leaders for continued professional development and leadership tune-ups. Companies have also figured out that it's more efficient to train their managers to be coaches than to hire external coaches, and some even provide in-house certification programs. Coaching has become an endemic part of the corporate world.

Leadership development has been explored for centuries in tens of thousands of books, and more recently on TEDx's, YouTube videos, podcasts, and blogs. Many have been written by familiar names such as Marcus Aurelius, Richard Branson, Brené Brown, Dale Carnegie, Stephen Covey, Daniel Goleman, Steve Jobs, Esther Perel, Sheryl Sandberg, Alan Sugar, Sun Tzu, Oprah Winfrey, Irvin Yalom, and Zig Ziglar. I humbly pay homage to them and so many other giants in the field. Uniformly, they agree that the soft skills required in leadership boil down to understanding and motivating yourself, understanding and inspiring other people, and cultivating and managing dynamic relationships.

What do exceptional leaders have in common? These trailblazers motivate others to be braver people and better employees. They bolster productivity, morale, and leadership development in their teams. Exceptional leaders see the bigger picture in meetings, conversations, and conflicts, both in content and process. They also balance creative problem-solving with pragmatic results. Most importantly, exceptional leaders are in the business of inspiring employees to be successful and developing future leaders. Accordingly, I firmly believe that all exceptional leaders are also great coaches.

Emotional intelligence is not new either. The concept was coined by B. Leuner in the 1960s and popularized by Daniel Goleman in the 1990s. Emotional intelligence actually comprises all the skills taught in group facilitation and therapy training, where group leaders are trained to hone their own and others' personal awareness and interpersonal development. They also learn how to process social dynamics, sharpen listening and asking skills, model risk-taking in communication, draw healthy boundaries, avoid blurring their own issues with those of the team members, and facilitate healthy conflict and power dynamics in the group. I love running group coaching and leadership training groups for this reason.

Emotional intelligence in leadership is the ability to understand and manage your own emotions and behaviors, others' emotions and behaviors, the dynamics between you and others, and your team's development and dynamics. Emotional intelligence is busy! Emotional intelligence, in a nutshell, is the awareness and management of yourself and others. It is not about being emotionally incontinent, but about being intelligent and doing intelligent things with everyone's emotions and behaviors. Simple definition, but no easy feat. The purpose of all that awareness and management is to facilitate the team and its members to be successful, happy, and productive. And it's not surprising that the concept and practice of emotional intelligence are heavily borrowed from group facilitation training.

Throughout this book, I will braid together strands from coaching, leadership, and emotional intelligence as we rethink how to approach all three. Tens of thousands of books have been written about these topics and generally tend to define each term similarly with slight variations. However, we intuitively and theoretically know what they are and what effective coaching, leadership, and emotional intelligence look like; what seems to make their study elusive is that they require a fine balance between art and science in their execution. I hope this toolkit in your hand will bring to light the practical and rational within that balance for your coaching leadership practice.

CHAPTER 1

LAY OF THE LAND

∞∞∞∞∞∞∞∞∞∞∞∞∞∞∞∞∞∞∞∞∞∞∞∞∞∞∞

What situations will you and your team encounter
where soft skills will be essential?

∞∞∞∞∞∞∞∞∞∞∞∞∞∞∞∞∞∞∞∞∞∞∞∞∞∞∞

Before we dive into the five distilled principles of coaching leadership, we need to first map out the territory where soft skills will be essential, no matter what size of team or type of industry. We'll first explore the three types of conversation killers that stifle successful communication and will work through concrete examples of how you can avoid these common pitfalls. Next, we'll think about the different ways tough conversations show up (i.e., conflicts and complaints) and will rethink the role that anger plays in the workplace. This leads to a template for how leaders can "do" conflict. Finally, we'll examine the four stages of development that all teams undergo where conversations—especially tough conversations—serve as the foundations for team dynamics.

CONVERSATION KILLERS

Your goal as a leader will always be to motivate and inspire yourself and your team to do better and be better. Good relationships are the bedrock of this goal and are facilitated by constructive conversations. Being able to communicate well is fundamental to successful leadership, so before we go any further, here's a quick rundown of some of the bad habits that sabotage conversations.

I see three dire mistakes in nearly every conversation. At first, it will be easier to spot these common pitfalls when you hear other people talk. Eventually, you will develop a finely tuned ear that can pick up these mistakes in your own conversations, too. This skill will prepare you to catch your own mistakes and model to your team how to have constructive conversations.

CONVERSATION KILLER #1: HIJACKING

Hijacking is when you steal someone else's airtime or attention. Whatever the other person is talking about somehow slides into something about you. What does "hijacking" a conversation look like? It's easy to spot from the outside. Here's an example of a WhatsApp group message thread that demonstrates this concept.

> **Sue:** Guess what guys, I'm going to be interviewed by the Channel 5 news tomorrow.
> **Tim:** Wow! That's exciting. Congrats. What's the interview about?
> **Liam:** Woohoo! I'm in the presence of a celebrity!
> **Tim:** What time? AM or PM?

Liam: Hey, could you wear a T-shirt with my business logo?

Tim: When did you get a business logo?

Liam: Duh, since I hired that marketing specialist. Cost me a fortune!

How quickly did Liam hijack Sue's news to make it about himself? Hijacking is also called stealing someone else's thunder or limelight. But sometimes hijacking shows up a bit more subtly.

Dan: I got the annual marketing brief to submit to the board. It's way more work than I thought and I've left it til the 11th hour.

Mike: Oh my god! That was assigned weeks ago. And I don't understand why the VP didn't ask me to do the brief? I'm the manager.

Dan: I don't know why she assigned it to me.

Mike: I'm so tired of being overlooked. You saw how they gave the global research gig to Jamie, when they know I'm the one who outlined the whole thing for her.

Instead of listening to Dan's problem, Mike made the conversation all about himself with "I" this and "I" that.

Here is an alternative conversation if Mike was not hijacking.

Dan: I got the annual marketing brief to submit to the board. It's way more work than I thought and I've left it til the 11th hour.

Mike: Tell me where you are with the brief. What do you need and how can I help?

Here's another example of hijacking:

> **Chris:** Hey! How was your weekend?
>
> **Patty:** It was grim. I worked all weekend on this pitch for our new client. I'm a bit frazzled. And to add to my stress, the new COO is coming to sit in!
>
> **Chris:** Yikes! Yeah...you and me both. You know that big clinic accreditation review I was telling you about? I had to work all weekend at the office. I'm pulling an all-nighter tonight AND tomorrow to make the Wednesday deadline. You know I have a one-on-one with that new COO on Thursday. What's she like?
>
> **Patty:** I don't know. I've not met her yet. Hey, I gotta get back to work.

On the surface, this may sound like a normal dialogue. If you dig a little deeper, though, you can see how Chris is hijacking Patty's narrative. Some may argue Chris was sharing his story to commiserate with Patty, but Chris isn't really interested in listening to Patty's situation. Chris hooks Patty with the pseudo-empathic "Yikes" and "Yeah..." then goes in for the "Your story reminds me of what bigger thing is happening to me, me, me!"

Chris might even say he was trying to comfort Patty by minimizing her situation in comparison to his story, which is worse. He may go as far as to argue he was feeling badly that Patty was so stressed and was trying to distract her. Regardless, it's still all about Chris and what he wants to know about the new COO and how he feels about his own troubles. Patty just got pushed aside and I bet she regrets engaging with Chris at all.

Alternatively, if Chris didn't make this conversation about him, it might sound like this:

> **Patty:** It was grim. I worked all weekend on this pitch for our new client. I'm a bit frazzled. And to add to my stress, the new COO is coming to sit in!
>
> **Chris:** What do you need to polish up the presentation? How much more do you need to do before it's due?

Hijacking, which can also sound like parallel monologues, is fine if you're engaged in small inconsequential chitchat, but what if Patty was in a position where she needed Chris to hear her vent or to talk things through? When someone shares their troubles with you, it's most likely because they need to be heard, not to be hijacked.

Hijacking happens even when you're apologizing.

> **Manager:** I've received numerous emails from you about the security policy you disagree with. You've also been rallying the team to push your agenda by phone and emails behind my back. And the boss called me to tell me about the emails she got from you accusing me of excluding you from our policy planning meetings. How do you think your behavior is affecting me and the team?
>
> **Employee:** I'm so sorry. I shouldn't have gone over your head. I didn't mean to get you into trouble with your boss. I'm just so used to things being expeditious in my previous job. And I was so upset about the policy and how it could seriously impact our campaign. Then I heard you guys were all meeting about it, and I wasn't invited.

The employee sounds like she's apologizing, but she's actually still focused on defending her behavior. She's completely sidelined how upset her manager is and hijacking the conversation to what she wants, what she can do, who she is, and how she used to be treated before. This is not an apology but an oblivious justification.

CONVERSATION KILLER #2: PROJECTING

A generic definition of projection is when you use your own experience as a lens to assume and understand the other person's experience. When you hear yourself or someone else say, "If I were you…" or "If I were in your position…," you know there's going to be some projection.

Pete and Cat are friends who met through a start-up business support forum. Cat quit her corporate job soon after she had her second child. Now that her kids are finally in school, she's developing a consulting start-up and revamping her career as a new entrepreneur. Pete is the primary breadwinner for his family and invested most of his savings to jump-start his own online business which, after 18 months, failed to take off and generate enough income. He and his co-founder have lost their motivation to continue.

> **Pete:** My business partner and I have exhausted every funding avenue and besides, we're no longer feeling excited. I'm feeling more dread every day. We've decided to step away from our business and we're both back on the job market, looking for steady income in tech.

Cat: Oh no, you can't quit now! You've come this far. I can't believe you're throwing in the towel! I know it's not easy, but you gotta get back on track. If I were in your position, I'd revamp your sales and marketing for your next funding round. I can show you.

Cat is projecting her own anxiety about failing onto Pete. She sees Pete's dilemma through her own lens: the fear or shame of quitting. The big difference is she has the financial means to persevere. Meanwhile, she's not listening to Pete's pain and disappointment. If we were to see it from another angle, she doesn't want Pete to feel down and demotivated. She wants to motivate Pete and get him back on track. Again, this is what she wants and is not necessarily what Pete needs.

Alternatively, this conversation could have gone differently if Cat was less focused on herself and more on Pete.

Pete: My business partner and I have exhausted every funding avenue and besides, we're no longer feeling excited. I'm feeling more dread every day. We've decided to step away from our business and we're both back on the job market, looking for steady income in tech.
Cat: You guys worked really hard together. How are you and your business partner going to close up shop?
or
What does the tech job market look like for you guys?
or
I'm sorry to hear that. How are you guys doing?

CONVERSATION KILLER #3: UNSOLICITED ADVICE

Sometimes unsolicited advice is subtle, and sometimes it is blatant and in your face. If you're entering a conversation with the intention to educate, enlighten, or change someone, you're not coaching or leading. You are imposing and bulldozing. If someone associates you with feelings of disregard, intrusion, and pressure, you've lost their desire to be led by you. Your intentions may be noble, but if advice is not solicited and welcomed, it's a trespass.

> **Edward:** Congrats, I heard you got a bump up in your take-home!
>
> **Sam:** Yeah, thanks. I wasn't sure if they had the budget for it, but I got crazy and asked for 15 percent. AND I got it!
>
> **Edward:** Well, that shows you should've asked for more. You should've started higher.
>
> **Sam:** Uh...Yeah, well.........uhm......hey, I need to pack up and get to a dinner engagement.

We can only imagine what Sam was thinking as he walked away from Edward. Who wants to be around someone who doesn't listen to how excited you are about a pay raise during a company budget restructuring? Clearly, Sam is valued, and the company was doing whatever it could to keep him.

Alternatively, if Edward wasn't so keen on trying to be clever or patronizing, the conversation could have gone like this:

Sam: Yeah, thanks. I wasn't sure if they had the budget for it, but I got crazy and asked for 15 percent. AND I got it!

Edward: Wow, that's fantastic! Well, it's not surprising. You've been closing some big deals lately.

Sam: Thanks. Hey, a few of us are going out for dinner and drinks to celebrate. Can you join us?

This example is also a reminder to think about the importance of timing in dishing out any kind of advice. If there's no room or time to change, keep it to yourself. What's the point of giving advice when the opportunity to change or improve has passed? Poorly timed advice can be as bad as or worse than the unsolicited kind and can leave people feeling demoralized. It can even be construed as passive-aggressive emotional sabotage. It's like giving someone job interview tips right after they've just bombed a very important interview.

Consider these questions before you plate up your advice:

> Did they ask for my advice?
> Is this the right time?
> How does what I want to say add value to this person/ situation?
> Am I just trying to impress them?
> How do I phrase my advice so it does not shame, demoralize, or impose?

In superficial or social chats, it may be inconsequential what and how things are said or by whom. For leaders, the consequences of what you say and how you say it are enormous and can make or break others' motivation and success.

There is definitely a time and place to advise, and that's mostly when you have a novice or someone who needs structure and if someone specifically asks for your advice.

HOW TO AVOID CONVERSATION KILLERS

It's easy as a leader to fall into these bad conversational habits of hijacking, projecting, and giving unsolicited advice. It is a myth that a leader is supposed to have all the answers. This is the time and place to let go of being right or doing it your way. You don't empower others by showing or telling them how right you are, how great your advice is, or by exerting control. You might impress them, but you certainly won't empower them.

The trick is not to just be a leader, but to be a coaching leader, which means facilitating other people's professional development and performance. Your goal is to respect the other person's competence and will to find their own solutions. Trust them to trust their own expertise to make and take their solutions. Remember, it's not what *you* know, it's what *they* know. I know this is where you roll your eyes and think, "That takes too long. It's so much quicker to tell them what to do." Telling them the answer may be a way out for you to alleviate your impatience and get them out of your office, not a real solution they can use now and later. Besides, no one likes to be told what to do. Do you? Your job as the coaching leader is to draw out answers. Switch the light on so they can either piece together the tools and knowledge they already have or figure out what they need to add to their toolbox.

Not all coaching leadership is non-directive. There are three situations when you need to step in to direct and instruct.

1. When there is urgency and a decision needs to be made very quickly.
2. When the employee is not yet trained up or needs a jump-start to get moving.
3. When teams are just forming and/or new team members need you to provide structure and guidance.

Facilitative skills in coaching leadership fall on a spectrum that ranges from non-directive to directive engagement.

Pull solutions from them

Non-Directive

Listening to understand with intent and without judgment, bias, or advice

Reflecting and articulating the other person's emotions or thoughts

Clarifying and summarizing what's being discussed

Asking solution-focused questions to raise awareness

Giving feedback or observation about behavior and process

Offering guidance without pushing

Making suggestions without telling them what to do

Giving advice

Instructing and telling

Directive

Push solutions to them

(Adapted. Myles Downey)

TOUGH CONVERSATIONS

Dialogues that arise from conflicts or complaints are by definition tough, for both the speaker and the listener. These conversations are tough because you take the risk of being the "bad guy" or the bearer of bad news and the one who has to deal with someone else becoming emotional. The onus is on you as the leader not only to initiate but to facilitate these conversations. Tough conversations also occur when you have to own up to your mistakes, disappointments, or disagreements.

Tough conversations can arise from conflict, but clumsy conversations can make things more precarious. Just as you would prepare for a job interview with many mock interviews and rehearse your presentation by writing it out and practicing it out loud, I offer the same suggestion for tough conversations. There is a huge difference in how you feel, think, and convey your message between a monologue in your head and verbalizing them out loud. Once you put a voice to something, it becomes more real and alive. Even if you don't have time, rehearsing a few initial phrases or key points out loud before the meeting will help reduce your nerves when you're actually in that meeting. Reducing your nerves or high emotions will leave space for you to manage the other person's emotional reaction as you deliver bad news, discipline or fire someone, or deal with complaints.

Conflict

Conflict is unfairly villainized, as it can be constructive and healthy and is a necessary force in team evolution and interpersonal relationship development. Conflict is a signal within or between people when an important need is not being met or when there are gaps between people's interests or expectations.

There are two basic types of conflict: overt and covert. Overt conflict is when needs, values, and views clash in a way that everyone can see. Covert conflict is festering, lingering tension in relationships and organizations due to unexpressed or unresolved disagreement.

While we tend to see the destructive aspects of conflict and may have been conditioned to believe that conflict should be avoided, we are not taught to see its positive aspects or to embrace its role in our teams. When conflict is addressed in a timely way (as early as possible), it can actually serve as a catalyst for building trust and a call for constructive action. Fundamentally, conflict is good for the development and evolution of any relationship and organization as long as it's addressed before emotions and imaginations take over and fester.

After all, what do we call discoveries or revolutions resulting from surges of energy, movement, excitement, and tension? They're called "breakthroughs," not "avoidthroughs," "calmthroughs," or "nicethroughs." We have "growing pains," not "growing ease." Conflict is a sign that there is a breakthrough or development hankering to happen. It's a cry for guidance and leadership. Nothing grows out of ennui or inertia. No person, relationship, or team grows without friction.

Sometimes conflict arises and is internalized. Internal conflict is the gap between your potential and where you are now. Look at the distance between what you are doing and your potential or ideal self. The degree of inner conflict or distress is an indication of the size of the gap between where you are now and where you're meant to be. If you're pursuing your potential and taking action towards what you're meant to be doing, you're in that nice flow with a small gap. Whenever you see someone who is unhappy or dissatisfied, you are most likely looking at someone who has a big gap between where they are now and where they are meant to be or what they're meant to be doing.

These internal conflicts can be projected onto others. If you're behind with your big deadlines and feel overwhelmed, you might become impatient or critical with other people's minor mistakes, creating tension around you to express the tension inside you. Since you were unable to recognize that you are actually angry with yourself for procrastinating, you've now blurred the boundaries between yourself and the other person by projecting your disappointment onto others' laziness or tardiness.

Complaints

If you, as a leader, believe that your team is so complete that no one could possibly have any complaints, you may be heading into conflict without even realizing it. A complaint that goes unexpressed or unheard will fester into quiet resentment, and resentment, if unacknowledged, will develop into bitterness and contempt. Once an annoyance rots all the way to contempt, we have reached a point where management is no longer possible, and someone ends up hurting or leaving.

I encourage everyone to complain but with one rule: No whining allowed! Complaining for the sake of complaining is whining, and that's just annoying. Complaining without a potential solution is an expression of powerlessness. Complaining with a personal agenda is manipulative and controlling. The end result is that you lose credibility and respect.

However, complaining with offerings of proactive suggestions and solutions is constructive and an open invitation for discussion. This is a win for everyone. When a constructive complaint is expressed and heard, small wounds can be treated before they fester into a huge gash of resentment and contempt. Holding things in until disappointment crystallizes into resentment is bad for one's mental and physical health, morale, and productivity. And once the resentment has decayed to contempt, relationships and teams turn toxic.

Constructive complaining is hope for conversation, productive bantering, diverse perspectives, and potential solutions. As a leader, be careful to avoid judging someone as whiner, nagger, or moaner. Once you judge them, you are emotionally hooked and lose your ability to listen or be objective.

Anger

Anger is my favorite emotion, because it's simultaneously complex and simple and comes in all sizes, shapes, and different shades of red. Sadly, it's usually misunderstood and unfairly treated. Although anger can be liable for most conflicts, complaints, and tough conversations, it's the emotion most people are afraid of in these situations. And yet, as a leader, you're expected to manage your own and others' anger. How do you manage something you don't understand? How do you manage something you are actively trying to avoid?

Expressions of anger are taboo or even prohibited in most public social situations, especially in the workplace. If it isn't handled correctly, it can have devastating consequences for a team. That being said, anger remains my favorite emotion, because it's colorful and fiery and can range from peppery all the way to volcanic. But, far from telling you how to avoid anger, I'm here to champion its appropriate expression as a healthy and cathartic practice. Once you get insight into where your anger comes from, you might not be as scared of it in yourself. And just as important, once you see what's underlying someone else's anger, you may not avoid it or the people who have anger. Heck, you might even lean into and love it, realizing it's really a kitten and not a lion. But first, let's explore this highly misunderstood emotion so that we can keep its claws from hurting anyone.

Tip of the Iceberg

Given how powerful anger is, it may be surprising to learn that it is actually a by-product of other smaller negative emotions that may pose a threat to our freedom, safety, or significance. Picture an iceberg with anger as the tip. Below the waterline are misunderstanding, disappointment, oppression, sadness, shame, fear, and related emotions such as helplessness and inadequacy. These emotions can lead us to feel insignificant, fragile, disrespected, small, frustrated, unheard, ignored, violated, and powerless; for some people, they will do whatever it takes to avoid feeling this way.

Anger can be seen as a "scapegoat emotion," because when we're not able to manage our sadness, shame, fear, or other related emotions that potentially make us feel small and helpless, those feelings can be inappropriately or understandably expressed as anger to potentially make us feel bigger, like puffing up our feathers. Anger may also be the result of unmet needs, such as freedom, safety, and significance. When someone is angry, it's a sure sign that one or more of their important needs is not being met.

Anger can occur because someone feels misunderstood, disrespected, or threatened. The catalyst behind most comic book superheroes stems from a place of overcoming powerlessness or compensating for weakness, which fires them up to champion for justice. How many superheroes do we know that were orphaned, insignificant, or helpless before they became rescuers and saviors? Let's look at the villains—yes, the more colorful nemeses of our superheroes. Villains get to act out their anger, and they do so because they fear losing their power and attention. Again, even villains' anger may be disguised to hide fear and vulnerability. Isn't it interesting that most villains wear masks or disguises? And most superheroes hide their alter ego, a mere human, a weakling.

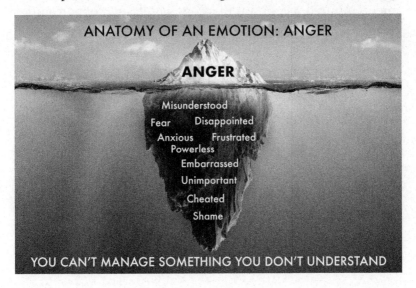

ANATOMY OF AN EMOTION: ANGER

ANGER

Misunderstood
Fear   Disappointed
Anxious   Frustrated
Powerless
Embarrassed
Unimportant
Cheated
Shame

YOU CAN'T MANAGE SOMETHING YOU DON'T UNDERSTAND

Constructive Anger

Anger can be used for good or evil. The constructive side of anger takes the form of passion, fervor, and excitement. The destructive side looks like rage and violence, and for some when this force gets suppressed it turns into withdrawal, apathy, or submission. When anger is used constructively, it stokes the fire to fight for what matters to you. For some, love and joy are what motivate them, while others are motivated by this flame, the exciting part of anger that activates them to fight, claw, conquer, and win. If something matters to the point of flaming passion, the threat of losing that could motivate people to proactively keep the fire alive.

Like our superheroes, we'd all like to use our fury to our advantage by using it positively to activate us into great action. Before we do that, let's understand it first. When someone is afraid of losing power or losing passion, know that anger may be a mask. Anger generally springs from emotions related to fear of not getting an important need met or fear of losing significance, opportunities, pride, attention, security, safety, etc.

Next time someone gets angry, take a step back to consider what need is not being met here. What could they be afraid of losing? Which vulnerable emotion(s) or state are they hiding behind this mask of anger? Powerlessness, embarrassment, invisibility, disrespect, helplessness, shame, loneliness, misunderstanding, inadequacy, etc.? Or simply ask, "What important need is not being met?" Anger gives the impression of power and is often used to compensate for a sense of weakness. I hope this twist on anger helps you to understand people who feel and express anger, instead of villainizing them. When a child throws a tantrum, you think to ask, "What's really going on? What do they need? Food? Nap? Reassurance?" Adults throw tantrums, too, don't we?

When you're angry, the fastest tactic to understanding yourself is to practice immediacy, recognizing and acknowledging the current state. Simply state the facts:

> "I feel angry/outraged/upset about (person/event). What I actually feel is (pick an emotion from below the waterline) about/by/in (person or event)."

> "I feel angry they didn't offer me the promotion. What I actually feel is disappointment and embarrassment that I didn't get it."

> "I feel outraged that Jake was so patronizing to me. What I feel is disrespected. Wait, what I actually feel is disappointed that I missed the chance to stand up for myself."

It's also more constructive to state "I feel angry" rather than "I am angry." The former objectifies anger and gives it distance, and it's something you are experiencing. The latter says that anger is who you are, implying it's a definitive identity. Like, I am tall, I am human, or I am an adult.

If you're too riled up to apply immediacy right away, give yourself a little time. Research studies on moods tell us it takes 10 to 20 minutes for us to emotionally cool off. Counting to 10 doesn't work. It takes a full coffee break or a walk or jog around the block to switch your moods. Once you've calmed down enough to fill in the blanks and see your below-the-waterline emotion, the insight may be enough to slow down the momentum of your anger. This also works when dealing with someone else who is inflamed with anger. Ask yourself, "What important need is not being met for them, and what else besides anger might they be feeling?" Once you figure that out, it becomes much easier to diffuse an angry outburst. One of the quickest ways to diffuse anger is to ask, "What do you need?" or "What can I do?"

Anger has a bad reputation for a good reason. If your anger boils without a release valve, you will explode, and explosions can do a lot of damage. If you are able to back up and identify what the initial underlying feeling is and how it could be related to a pain point, sadness, shame, or fear, you've found your release valve. Go behind the mask and deal with the feeling of weakness or defeat, which may be difficult but not as tough as dealing with anger head on.

With practice, you'll understand your triggers better so that you can anticipate your reactions and, in turn, put yourself in a better position to shift your patterns of behavior. Ask:

> What have I accomplished with my anger?
> How can I react differently next time?
> Is this the way I want to be seen?
> What else can I do to release this angry energy?

You've just been promoted internally to lead the team you were a member of for the last three years. One of your team members started coming in late to staff meetings. Her tardiness is turning into a running joke. You have had a conversation with her about punctuality and respecting other people's time, but she still continues to be late. The pattern of tardiness beyond this point is construed as passive-aggressive anger. What is she gaining by being late? What is she trying to express? What does she need? She makes people laugh by her tardiness and she gets attention. Power? She gets to test the boundaries to see how far you will tolerate her act of rebellion/envy. Fear? She's going to lose you as a friend, now that you're no longer peers. Resistance? She may feel she should have applied for the team lead role but couldn't pluck up the courage. But you did. Or she's not ready to accept this change in roles.

Questions to ask her during your next meeting with her:

> What are you gaining from being late to our meetings?
> How do you think we could interpret your pattern of being late to the last five out of seven meetings?
> What's the impact on the team when you behave this way?
> How are you managing this shift in roles?
> It's awkward for me, and these are the reasons why…

In a nutshell, even when we know that it is not good or right, we still get angry. Anger is a distraction, a disguise, or a substitute for unmet needs or fragility. Anger serves a purpose and sometimes becomes a reward. When you express anger or lash out, you get attention. Anger temporarily relieves tension and can give the impression of power. It disguises weakness.

DO CONFLICT

Constructive and open conversation is never more crucial than when there is conflict. Few people are very good at dealing with conflict. Too many avoid it, like they avoid anger, and wish that it would somehow just go away. The biggest obstacle to facing conflict is the fear of an explosion or a fight. Psychologically, we may avoid conflict because of a perceived loss: loss of face, respect, status, being liked, comfort zone, or something else meaningful. The irrational logic is that if we avoid the conflict, we can avoid dealing with the potential or perceived loss. For example, you avoid telling your team how disappointed you have been with their performance. Rather than have this honest conversation with your team members, you invite trainers to conduct time management and team building workshops. You avoid radical candor because you don't want to lose your popularity and convivial office environment. You worry that if you have the "shape up or ship out" talk, you will offend them, they won't like you, and the atmosphere will be awkward. In reality, honesty may be the one thing they need from you, and attending more workshops and playing team building games will not address the root of the issues.

When we're faced with a stressful situation, we tend to respond with fight or flight. I have often observed another type of response, "freak and freeze," where you're freaking out on the outside while you freeze up on the inside. You try to turn the volume off, go numb, or pray the conflict will go away. None of these responses are healthy or helpful. Here's another option: *do* conflict. You have a choice. You can avoid conflict and teach others you cannot be trusted when things get messy, or you can be braver and face the tension to learn from the differences, discord, and tough conversation. Decide what's more important to you: having their respect or avoiding conflict.

Great leaders know that conflict is where real growth can happen. Embrace the discomfort of conflict to better see where things aren't working. I know it sounds counterintuitive. To use my first skydiving lesson as an example, as I was about to jump out of the plane for the first time, my instructor shouted over the loud propeller engine noise, "Okay, remember to open up your body and raise your arms up and legs back!" Whaaat? Of course, my first instinctual response was to curl up into a fetal position as I jumped. It felt counterintuitive, but the more I opened up the more control I had.

To approach conflict as a coaching leader, you choose courage to acknowledge and call it out. Fear is a reaction; courage is a choice. Figure out what you are afraid of losing. Your fear is the reaction to a potential loss you want to avoid. Clarifying your potential loss will help you take one step away from your fear of the conflict or tension. This step can give you the perspective you need to accept the conflict and keep you from getting too emotional or afraid. Remember, it's a privilege when someone needs you to listen to them, even if they are complaining or in a state of conflict, because it means there is trust and hope. The first thing you do in a time of any conflict is to listen. This prevents you from reacting and calms the other person down. Bear witness to their troubles without getting entangled in the drama with your reaction.

Here are three quick simple steps to address conflict objectively as a leader.

1. <u>Listen</u>. They need to be seen and their stories need to be heard.
   What's going on?
   What's happening?
   Will you tell me more about...?
   What do you see as the real problem?

2. <u>Ask</u>. You find out what they need by asking short questions that move people from conflict to calm.
   What do you need?
   What would a solution look like?
   What if you can't have that/do that, what else could work?
   What can I do?
   What can you do?

3. <u>Give</u> clear and objective observation or feedback if steps 1 and 2 don't help the other person to come to their own realization. Summarize the information you gathered from listening and asking. You can either do this in the moment, if that is possible, or you can set up another meeting in the near future if you or they need more time to digest what you uncover in steps 1 and 2. When you give your feedback, provide objective observations of the relevant events, behaviors, or performance rather than offering judgment or interpretation of their motives. Ensure the feedback is something actionable, something they

can think about that will lead to something they can do. This discussion will include your expectations of what to resolve and how to resolve it, how they can improve their performance, or what the end goal could look like.

Steps 1–3 can be used to facilitate discussions with the aim of finding agreement on actions to move forward through learning from conflict.

FOUR STAGES OF TEAM DEVELOPMENT

Whether we're talking about a professional situation or a personal one, every relationship or team development will go through the following stages proposed by Bruce Tuckman in 1965. Being able to anticipate the team's developmental dynamics will give you a heads-up on managing yourself and others on the team. Knowing that the thunder claps after you see the lightning strike prevents you from being surprised by the rumble.

FORMING
How do I fit in? What are we doing here? What's our plan?

Forming is the honeymoon stage where everyone is distracted by the novelty of something new: new team, new project, or new member or leader. Everyone is on their best behavior. At this initial juncture, everyone arrives neat and polite and colors within the lines (socially speaking). Everyone looks around to see how they might fit within the team and tries to ascertain whether the others in the team are safe and trustworthy. During this stage, teams may not be particularly productive. If there's a disagreement during this stage, people are more likely to yield and tolerate.

Every dyad or team lingers in the forming stage until a sufficient amount of time has passed without change in its membership. The amount of time depends on how quickly members jockey for position or leadership and the team's threshold for inertia. Teams tend to reset every time a member leaves the circle or someone new enters. This is why teams with high turnover get stunted, disrupting productivity. As long as the team remains in this "is it safe and do we fit?" stage, there is a whole lot of polite exchange but no development of real trust yet. Getting stuck here creates a false sense of security. Getting along is mistaken for cohesion. Politeness is mistaken for respect.

All that niceness and inertia have a limit. Diverse ideas and methods are dynamic, creative solutions are messy, and innovation is provocative. Differences can sometimes feel threatening. All this diverse energy leads to storming. Trust is knowing you or the team will be robust through problems and trouble. Nobody wants fair-weather friends, leaders, or team members. Organically, developing teams and growing relationships within it will test themselves to see if they can survive and thrive in times of conflict and mess.

As the leader, you will need to provide some guidance and direction initially because the team identity is not clear yet. Member roles have not been established, and the communication patterns have not been tried and tested.

STORMING

What's everyone's role? Who's taking charge? This may not work!

Storming is usually a reliable sign the team or the organization needs to move out of its comfort and snooze zone and is ready to progress to the next level where real decisions can be made. Roles are unclear and team relationships are still blurry. The purpose of the team has to be confirmed. This stage is marked by provocation or perturbation, but it doesn't have to take the form of a big or dramatic conflict. Storming is also the time when team members try out if and how they fit in on their team. For example, you or your team members may have a moment of disagreement, resistance, rebellion, or complaint, signaling diverse ideas and a readiness to grow and learn from these differences. As the leader, regard this tension as the abrasive that polishes the surface, the growing pain, and the potential breakthrough. It's a necessary stage if you want your team to rely on each other to deal with conflict now and in the future.

The storming stage is the time to test the team's level of trust, resilience, strength, and commitment. It is a time when team members get to try out their voices and take risks, and it's when your rationality, patience, and listening skills will be summoned. Brace yourself. This stage is where you practice being more comfortable with your own inner conflict and mess. One of the simplest ways to address the storming stage is to neutrally acknowledge the tension in the moment, a technique that is also called immediacy (a concept we will delve into later in the book). When you see there is tension in the team or between two people, you call it out and ask a question that moves towards a solution, such as "Looks like we've reached a stalemate, what could we do about that?" or "We're avoiding the elephant in the room, how do you want to deal with that before we move on?" Just by calling it out without analysis or explanation, others will see that you are not afraid of the mess and want to clean things up together. Timely identification of any misunderstanding or tension will prevent unexpressed views that lead to blowups and passive-aggressive attitudes later. In times of conflict, what are you teaching your team about you? Are you an avoider, a blamer, or an honest leader who may be afraid but still steps up to lead them?

Show your team how to "visit" with or ride out the storm together by first acknowledging the conflict and then inviting them to describe, resolve, or cope with it. If nothing else, show them you are courageous enough to visit with this uncomfortable guest. You don't need to have the answers, just the courage to ask the questions to move things along. For example, "There seem to be issues about the workload. What do you need to make things fairer or manageable? What's realistic? What can I do?" Sometimes, they may just need to be heard, even if there is no definitive solution. Visiting or weathering the storming stage together will help the team to evolve to the next stage: norming.

Storming is natural and par for the course for every successful relationship, team, and organization. If you anticipate the storms, you can prepare for them so that you're not caught by surprise. Mishandling—or worse, ignoring—these situations ultimately destroys teams and team members' trust that you will have their back when things get tough.

As the leader, your task is to sell or clarify the vision or goal of the group or project. You may need to be braver to endure tension to facilitate conflict that may dominate this stage.

NORMING
What are our expectations and rules? How can we work together?

In the norming stage, roles are clarified, relationships are either implied, assumed, or made explicit, and team goals are agreed upon and mutually understood. If you've identified, accepted, and teased out the conflict through the storming stage, everyone will have earned their roles and learned the rules within the team. Welcome to the rules and tools stage.

Storming and norming often go hand in hand or occur simultaneously, so I tend to clump them together. For example, you absentmindedly say something offensive to your colleague during a meeting. She assertively and sensitively tells you she thought what you said was rude. You first feel defensive then realize she may be right and curiously ask the others if that came across as rude. Most agree it was. You apologize for being a cr*ass*. This exchange files away a norm that members can be sensitive, assertive, express themselves, take a survey, and even discuss a difficult issue. And it's okay to sensitively call each other out.

How you and the team manage the storm dictates the norms. If you avoid it, the rules are clear to everyone that the team will similarly duck and dive to evade it. If you skip the storming stage and fake your way into the norming stage, walking on eggshells becomes the rule. Don't mistake smiles and nods for working well together, when in reality it may be glossed-over conflict or apathy. Absence of conflict does not equal harmony.

Some teams regress from storming back to forming if they delay dealing with tension and conflict. For example, a team member might lose their temper during a discussion, then apologize after the meeting and bring a box of cupcakes the next day. Instead of addressing the outburst, the team might act like nothing happened and happily enjoy the regressive pastry. In this case, contrition by cupcakes is a cop-out and is a dysfunctional norm.

Norming is the stage when everyone teaches everyone else how to work more effectively with each other. This is the stage when the team learns what is acceptable and what is not. On a successful and cohesive team, people learn that being late to meetings, dismissing or deriding someone's idea, interrupting someone, and monopolizing meetings are unacceptable practices. However, questioning or challenging each other's ideas, including the leader's, is acceptable (as long as they are directed at the idea, not the person). Once norms are in place, your team grows to the next stage: performing.

During this stage, you will recognize who is a team player, who is a follower, and who has natural leadership tendencies. Observe people's natural learning and problem-solving styles. As a leader, your task is to support and also to join in to develop interpersonal norms in the team. You can also be the process observer for how the team reaches or tries out rules and roles. For example, "I notice Tom likes to think out loud, and Greg tends to think things through before speaking." Now you will also think twice before pairing Tom and Greg for assignments; Tom will drive Greg nuts with all that external processing and misunderstand Greg's pensiveness as agreement.

PERFORMING
Shared goals. Risk-taking. Accountability. Creative problem-solving.

Commitment to the goal or team's performance gets established here. The team can start getting creative and strategic about working well together. Once everyone has taught each other how to see and relate with each other, they can grow and mingle as a team and move to the performing stage. Having agreed on the lay of the land with members knowing their roles and expectations and the rules of conduct, now the team can get into step with the projects at hand or the task of functioning as a working team. Rinse and repeat. Having been through the rewards of making it to the performing stage, the team may feel a bit more comfortable next time about a few more storms and norms to get back to performing.

If there has been a glitch in the norming stage or dysfunctional norms have been adopted, the team will eventually regress to storming to reset itself. Trust the organic group process that every team *wants* to work well together.

Every time there is a change, the team will re-form, re-storm, and re-norm, organically cycling and recycling through the stages as it develops. The change can be due to new projects, workload, new members, colleagues becoming bosses, consultants temporarily joining the team, layoffs, etc. The most recent example of change was the shift to working from home due to the COVID-19 pandemic. Teams went straight into storming until we found a way to norm as our homes quickly became our offices, schools, and entertainment centers. Once everyone recovered from the shock, grieved the old normal, and stormed, we had to find rules and roles for our new *normal*.

As a leader, your task is easy at this stage. You get to empower and delegate and keep your and the team's eyes up front until the team or the project needs to adjourn to the next project, membership change, or the team disbands.

Regardless of how the relationship or team shifts, turns, or revolves in and out of forming, storming, norming, and performing, these moves occur through conversations between people. In particular, tough conversations serve as linchpin moments that can define team dynamics and productivity.

CHAPTER 1 KEY POINTS

- You can't manage something you don't understand. Understand first, then manage.
- Leaders need soft skills to navigate common terrain that all teams will encounter.
- Three common types of conversation killers to avoid are hijacking, projecting, and offering unsolicited advice.
- Contrary to common practice and belief, anger has an important role to play in the workplace when harnessed appropriately.
- Doing conflict involves choosing courage, listening, asking, and giving clear and honest observation or feedback.
- Teams evolve through four stages of development: forming, storming, norming, and performing, where storming is pivotal.

CHAPTER 2

INTRODUCTION TO FIVE CORE PRINCIPLES

~~~~~~

How can soft skills strengthen your coaching leadership?

~~~~~~

We have identified the most common obstacles and pitfalls to effective communication in teams; let's now dive into the five core principles to help you and your team thrive. This list is meant to be an easy reference and can help reframe your mindset in the midst of a crisis or refresh your psychological stance as you enter a situation where you're being called on as a coaching leader. We'll tackle each of these principles in depth in the following chapters.

CLEAN YOUR BOUNDARIES

We can date the importance of knowing thyself all the way back to the days of Socrates. Being aware of and managing your emotions and behaviors sound simple, but clearly, it's not so easy to achieve. Modern-day scholars and scientists are still proposing it as one of the vital skills for success and happiness. I think Socrates would be proud that we haven't given up on self-awareness and we continue to be works in progress.

For successful leadership, there must be a clear emotional boundary between you and the other person. Be clear about where you end and where the other person begins. This healthy boundary only happens when you're self-aware about the good, the bad, and the ugly of what makes you tick. Observe and educate yourself about yourself, how you come across to other people, and how others affect your thoughts and behavior. Study yourself as a subject, so you know yourself well enough to think before you feel, speak, or act.

Self-awareness is the gateway to making informed decisions about yourself and other people around you, especially the ones you lead. Be intelligent about your and others' emotions. Having knowledge about how and why you have certain biases, opinions, and reactions, and why and how your buttons are pushed help you understand your behavior, perspective, and reality. When you know what your "stuff" is, then you're able to distinguish them from other people's "stuff."

Self-awareness also ensures that you stay in your lane and you can help other people to stay in theirs, so that there is a clear line between you and them. These lines are boundaries. A clean boundary also means that you're clear about what your responsibilities, issues, and needs are, separating them from the other person's responsibilities, issues, and needs. Simply put, your reality is not theirs, and their reality is not yours. Blurred boundaries can get a lot of leaders into trouble. For example, they're socially too familiar with the people they evaluate, they project their own ideals and expectations onto others, they over-empathize and get emotionally hooked, or they take on more responsibilities because they don't know how to draw the line to delegate.

FOCUS AND LISTEN

Active listening is often misunderstood and mis-practiced as "overactive" listening. Your mind is busy trying to connect the dots using your own experiences and lens as a reference point to understand the other person. Most mistakes in communication are made here. You get too wrapped up with interpreting what's being said and lose focus on what the speaker is actually saying. Overactive listening occurs when you let yourself fill in the blanks and end up jumping to conclusions, making snap judgments, or overanalyzing motives. You get seduced by why something happened rather than focusing on listening to what's really being said.

Focused listening is not about you and how you have to analyze and know how they feel and think. Rather, it's about you focusing on the other person and letting them show you how they understand, using their own lens. Put your lens away. Focused listening is about you stepping down in order for the other person to step up and speak. Get out of your own way and put your issues away so that you can focus and listen to others. Listening is about how present you are for them so that they feel heard. It's less about what you understand, and more about what they understand from talking.

DO RATIONAL EMPATHY

When you have a genuine interest in making time and giving your undivided attention for someone to speak, empathy naturally occurs. However, it's impossible to *exactly* know, understand, or feel what someone else is experiencing. That's okay. When you're busy or stressed, it's difficult to quickly decipher someone else's feelings and thoughts and then to emotionally align with them. As with focused listening, "doing" empathy is less about you scrambling and reaching to understand, but more about letting the other person be heard. It's about you pausing to be present for them, giving them airtime. That's where your focus should stay if you're short on feeling empathy. Sometimes bearing witness to their narrative is all they need.

Some people are naturally empathic, while others genuinely struggle to see things from someone else's perspective and to find their own corresponding feelings. When you don't have the capacity, nature, or patience to *feel* empathy, it's still possible to *do* empathy. Doing empathy starts with accepting the other person's thoughts, feelings, and experiences as their own. Your job is to set aside any notion of how you want them to be or how they should be. Set aside the well-meaning "I should know what's best for them" or "I need to know what they're going through." Instead, take yourself out of the equation and let them teach you about their experience. If you don't understand or don't have the emotional energy to care about their views, then care about the fact that they care about their views. This is rational empathy. The focus is still on them and caring that they care.

ASK MOVING QUESTIONS

Ask questions not just to uncover content but also to find ways to help people move forward. Your curious and moving questions demonstrate that you are listening, engaged, and interested. An added bonus is that your questions can reflect how curious and intelligent you are. Your questions can either fan the flame or calm the fire in the other person. The best solutions to their problems are those they make and take on their own. You don't like being told what to do, and no one else does either. Facilitate or clarify the other person's stories, ideas, views, and approaches by asking *what* and *how* rather than *why*. What and how questions focus on the present and future, while the why questions keep you in the past. Teach people that you care and dare enough to ask solution-focused and sometimes difficult questions.

Even as you listen, it's common courtesy to ask for permission to enter someone's thinking space. For example, "Do you need me to just listen?" or "Could I ask questions?" or "Do you need me to give suggestions and solutions?"

DO IMMEDIACY

This is the golden intervention that will help you survive and thrive in times of conflict and other awkward, sticky moments that life presents. This is what you do when your mind defies you and you feel clueless. Immediacy means immediately reflecting, clarifying, or asking about what is going on here and now. Instead of avoiding that mistake or an awkward moment, you call it what it is.

Uh, that was awkward.
Looks like we're at a crossroad.
I didn't mean it the way it sounded.
Did you say it the way I heard it?
Could we start this conversation over?
Okay, that was embarrassing.

Simple immediacies like these get you more credibility than any elaborate intervention, because they are honest and in the moment. Any tension, when acknowledged and experienced together, may open doors. Be braver and control the moment with immediacy.

CHAPTER 2 KEY POINTS

These five core principles will help you and your team thrive:

1. Clean your boundaries: Draw the emotional and social line between you and the other person.

2. Focus and listen: Step down so the other person has space to step up and speak. Step down, listen up.

3. Do rational empathy: Bear witness to their story, their way.

4. Ask moving questions: Care and dare enough to ask difficult questions that will help them move forward and upward.

5. Do immediacy: Survive and thrive in tough and awkward moments by acknowledging and addressing them immediately.

CHAPTER 3

CLEAN YOUR BOUNDARIES

How can you harness self-awareness to create and
maintain boundaries essential to effective leadership?

SELF-AWARENESS

The key to creating a good relationship with someone you lead is for you to have clear boundaries between where you end and where the other person begins. And the key to creating good boundaries is self-awareness. The better you know yourself and what makes you tick, the better you can untangle your own thoughts and emotions from other people's. The ability to distinguish between what issues or needs belong to you and what issues and needs belong to another person is a foundational skill in any successful relationship.

For example, there is a popular manager who is appreciated and rated highly for how she maintains a sense of community for her team. A new employee joins the team. He's very independent and seen as socially aloof. He rarely joins in on the monthly happy hour the manager enjoys coordinating to help the team bond. She is increasingly annoyed by his absence and distance. And her ego is bruised because he doesn't appreciate, let alone notice, her efforts to fold him into the team. However, once she separates her need to be liked from his need for autonomy, it'll be easier for her to accept his aloofness as part of his independent-mindedness and not a reflection on her. His aloofness has nothing to do with her.

When my clients start to emotionally blur their needs with someone else's business or problem, I say, "It's nacho cheese." (It's not your cheese.) And they know I mean it's not their job to fix other people or give unsolicited advice. Your need to be right or to teach doesn't mean other people want or need to learn from you.

Self-awareness is not about gazing at your navel. Besides, *too much* navel-gazing can distract us from focusing on what we really need to do: get our work done and move things forward. Self-awareness entails spotting things about yourself without irrational judgment and at least accepting them, even if you don't understand them. These may even be traits you don't like about yourself. You're able to spot your reactions, judgments, biases, and motives and know how these affect you. More importantly, you are aware of how they affect others around you. Also, when you're self-aware, you're able to both understand and manage your reactions.

How do you learn to control your feelings and gain an understanding of how your emotions affect you and other people? There are several different strategies to achieve this. One is neutral observation of how you feel and think. Some people refer to it as the "balcony view" of the drama. In the same way that you suspend judgment of other people when you empathize with them, you do the same for yourself. There is nothing woo-woo or fuzzy about this; you are simply taking a distant view. Observing yourself from a detached, nonjudgmental perspective is what enables you to know what's your stuff and how your stuff affects you and other people.

A tangible and proven strategy for developing self-awareness is keeping a mind-dumping journal. In a notebook or on your computer, divide your page into two columns, use the left side to pour out all your thoughts, biases, feelings, and reactions about things, people, and events—anything on your mind. Unburden your mind. A few days or weeks later, return to your mind-dumped pages and use the right side to jot down any reactions, questions, revelations, or thoughts on what you wrote on the left. You may find patterns or surprises. You don't have to write every day. You don't have to write in paragraphs; use bullet points or make lists of what's going on in your mind. It can be a mind map or in pictures. It may be messy and disjointed, like your natural thoughts and feelings. Mind-dump to free up space in your mind. One of my clients calls it her Dumping Diary, and this DD helps her to do her own self-coaching.

Finally, you can elicit other people's views of you. Ask for candid feedback from your friends, family, coach, or colleagues. Make sure you respect and trust them. Teach them how to give feedback so you don't burden them with a lengthy 360-degree feedback or with a loaded "so, what do you think about me?" These are sample questions to use or rephrase to suit your own style, to make it easier for them:

> What adjectives would you use to describe me?
> When I'm stressed, how do I behave?
> What is it like for you to be around me when I'm stressed like that?
> What annoys you about me?
> How can you tell when I'm trying to hide my annoyance?
> How do I express my negative emotions? Positive emotions?
> How do you know if I'm upset about something?
> If I were to be featured on the cover of a magazine, (use this with creative friends)
>> which magazine would it be?
>> what would be the headlines?
>> what would be sample titles of featured articles?
>> what would be the subtitles?
>> what would the cover highlight about me?

The main purpose of self-awareness for coaching leaders is to maintain clean boundaries between you and the people you lead. This ensures that you can check your baggage at the door before entering the room to help others with their baggage.

VALUES

Your core values are the gears that outline your life and work purpose, make up your moral compass, and inform your personal and professional goals. When you or the current situation goes against them, you may feel stressed, discontent, conflicted, or despondent. So, identifying your values is an essential step towards self-awareness. To jump-start the process of narrowing down your values, ask yourself a few of these sample questions:

> What fires me up?
> What gets me out of bed in the morning?
> What are my top drivers that motivate me?
> What do I respect about myself, and why?
> What do I stand for?
> What are my strong beliefs or principles I won't give up?
> I have no tolerance for _____.

Your key skills as a coaching leader include knowing your needs so you can set them aside to avoid mixing them up with the other person's needs. This keeps your boundaries clean and allows you to help others without inadvertently trying to meet your own needs.

You will likely have different values that drive you at work and at home. Below is a list of work values. Choose 20 that are essential to you and use them to describe what you stand for at work and as a leader. From those 20, choose 10 that are a bit more important than the other 10. You are now left with your top 10 values that structure and inform your needs, drivers, and motivation. From those 10, choose 5 that you absolutely cannot and will not compromise. These top 5 values describe the core of what you stand for. These are your core drivers about why you're doing what you do, and these will activate and sustain you. If these don't reflect what you do or how you are at work, this incongruency may be the reason for your dissatisfaction. (You can use this list to do the same exercise for your home life.)

CORE VALUES LIST

Abundance	Exhilaration	Making a Difference
Encouragement	Joy	Spirit
Inspiration	Sensitivity	Clarity
Respect	Balance	Fascination
Acceptance	Experience	Mastery
Endurance	Justice	Spontaneity
Integrity	Sensuality	Commitment
Sacrifice	Being the Best	Fearlessness
Achievement	Expertise	Motivation
Energy	Kindness	Stability
Intelligence	Serenity	Community
Safety	Belonging	Financial Independence
Acknowledgement	Exuberance	Open-Mindedness
Enjoyment	Knowledge	Stamina
Intellectual Stimulation	Significance	Competitiveness
Satisfaction	Camaraderie	Fitness
Adaptability	Fairness	Optimism
Enthusiasm	Leading the Field	Status
Intensity	Simplicity	Confidence
Security	Capability	Flexibility
Adventure	Faith	Organization
Excellence	Learning	Strength
Intuition	Sincerity	Contribution
Self-control	Certainty	Focus
Ambition	Fame	Originality
Excitement	Loyalty	Structure
Investing	Sociability	Control
Self-reliance	Challenge	Freedom
Assertiveness	Family	Passion

Success	Power	Identity
Cooperation	Trust	Reflection
Fun	Determination	Winning
Perceptiveness	Happiness	Emotional Intelligence
Support	Preparedness	Imagination
Courage	Trustworthiness	Relaxation
Generosity	Dignity	Wisdom
Perseverance	Harmony	Empathy
Synergy	Proactivity	Impartiality
Creativity	Uniqueness	Reliability
Giving	Discipline	Wonder
Persistence	Health	Independence
Taking Risks	Professional Identity	Resilience
Credibility	Unique Selling Point	Youthfulness
Grace	Diversity	Insightfulness
Persuasiveness	Honesty	Resourcefulness
Teamwork	Professionalism	Zaniness
Curiosity	Variety	
Gratitude	Drive	(Adapted. Scott Jeffrey's
Planning	Honor	Core Values List)
Thankfulness	Progression	
Daring	Vision	
Gregariousness	Education	
Playfulness	Humility	
Tolerance	Punctuality	
Decisiveness	Vitality	
Growth	Effectiveness	
Pleasure	Humor	
Travel	Recognition	
Dependability	Wealth	
Guidance	Efficiency	

YOU ARE IMPERFECT

If you're in a position to help others, then position yourself to help. You don't have to be perfect to help other people. Besides, perfection is overrated. It's rigid, brittle, and unattainable. Even if, let's say, you reach perfection, then what next?

Be true to your flaws. If you're a bit arrogant, know that you tend to intimidate or put certain people off and be prepared to accept that some people won't like you. If you're moody, acknowledge it and recognize that when emotions are high, it's not the best time to make big and important decisions or take impulsive action. If you're vain, find humor in it. Do this self-searching behind proverbial closed doors and take the time to look at your naked self, as emotionally or rationally as possible. This can only strengthen you as a leader, because you're less likely to unconsciously carry the effects of your faults and unresolved issues to the office and be caught off guard.

BIASES

We all like to think that we are aware, open-minded, and unbiased and that we would never judge certain people or situations inappropriately. But unless you were raised in a social vacuum, biases are an inevitable part of being human. Identify and acknowledge your biases so you can leave them outside the meeting room when you lead and facilitate your team.

An older white male client recently said to me, "We're polar opposites. I'm not sure how you can help me." I'm a younger

Asian American female, and he's not. I entered the conversation aware that this was a big button just waiting to be pushed.

I replied, "Thank you for your candor. You're right, we are very different, and it seems that you're concerned about how I can understand you. Tell me, you've been with this company for 11 years and before that you worked at another for 10. In your experience, how did you do business with customers and colleagues who were very different from you? And what worked for you?"

He talked about his working style, leadership approach, struggles, and successes with diverse teams and customers. In other words, he talked himself out of his bias about our differences being a problem. Building on this disclosure, I then asked him if he would give me the same benefit of the doubt he gave his customers and colleagues to see if we could work together.

When clients ask questions about differences, they're usually not concerned with what's overt. They're asking about something deeper, such as whether the relationship will provide safety, trust, or worth. It may be a blunt question that disguises vulnerability.

Even though I could have defended myself with my credentials and experience, I kept myself out of the equation. I avoided getting hooked because I knew he wasn't asking about me or asking me to prove myself. This was a storming moment, and we were teaching each other how we could potentially work together. If I had been overactive in my listening and focused on myself by being defensive, the noise in my head would have drowned out what he really said and needed.

EMOTIONAL TEMPERATURE

If our values and imperfections are climate, emotional temperature is the weather. What makes you happy, sad, angry, afraid, and ashamed? What brings you joy and laughter, and what triggers feelings of fear or guilt? Being able to quickly ascertain your present emotional state can go a long way in creating separation from your triggers, baggage, and biases so you can be clear and present for those you lead.

If you look at the table below, you'll see there are five basic emotions, with each ranging from high to low intensity. Did you notice there is only one positive emotion? The other four are seen and experienced as negative, but more importantly, they are protective and warning emotions. They tell us when something is dangerous, unhealthy, or unsafe and keep us from being happy, which is the one state to which we all aspire. When something doesn't feel right or good, it's generally a cue for you to rethink how you need to see it to change your mood or attitude. For example, how are you distinguishing between what's good versus not bad, or not good versus bad. That fine line can result in a big difference in how you use your words to shift your thoughts and emotions, to swing your attitudes, and to change the action you take. This list is useful to gauge if a situation requires an impassioned reaction or just a footnote-sized response.

5 Basic Emotions	HAPPY	SAD	ANGRY	AFRAID	ASHAMED
HIGH	Ecstatic Elated Excited Overjoyed Exuberant Thrilled Fired up Passionate	Depressed Agonized Alone Hurt Dejected Hopeless Sorrowful Miserable	Enraged Furious Outraged Boiling Irate Seething Loathsome Betrayed	Terrified Horrified Scared stiff Petrified Panicky Frantic Shocked Threatened	Worthless Disgraced Dishonored Sorrowful Remorseful Defamed Mortified Admonished Devastated
MID	Cheerful Gratified Good Relieved Satisfied Glowing	Heartbroken Lost Distressed Somber Let Down Melancholy	Upset Mad Defended Frustrated Agitated Disgusted	Anxious Frightened Fearful Insecure Uneasy Intimidated	Apologetic Unworthy Sneaky Guilty Embarrassed Secretive
LOW	Glad Contented Pleasant Tender Pleased Mellow	Upset Unhappy Moody Blue Disappointed Dissatisfied	Perturbed Annoyed Uptight Resistant Irritated Touchy Disappointed	Apprehensive Cautious Nervous Worried Timid Unsure	Bashful Regretful Uncomfortable Pitied Silly

(Adapted. Julia West from Bradberry Greaves, 2009)

Notice how you respond to stressors and stimuli. Don't stop at "I'm stressed." Go into a deeper analysis.

> What are my stress triggers?
> When I feel stressed, how do I soothe this reaction?
> What does my stress relief say about me?
> What are other reactions or emotions that would describe what's going on with me?
> What's really bothering me? Losing control? Fear of failure?

For example, know the difference between being annoyed and furious at a team member's mistake, between being ecstatic and secretly pleased when you beat the competition, and between being disappointed and devastated by a project failure. If your reaction is out of proportion to the size of the situation, that is an alarm to you that there is something else going on with you beneath the surface. You go off the handle when your assistant sends you the wrong file by mistake before an important negotiation. Rationally, you know everyone makes mistakes. But this time, you may be projecting your frustration at yourself for leaving things until the last minute, and procrastination is something you've been seriously struggling with since college.

If you have tendencies to respond at the high end of the chart in the province of a drama queen/king or control freak (by the way, there's a huge overlap between the two!), don't worry. Observe and educate yourself about these tendencies. Know that you have a choice between low, mid, or high responses, and you're choosing the dramatic response. Ask self-coaching questions. Are you really enraged or just annoyed when things don't go as you planned or they don't go your way? Just because it's someone else's way doesn't mean it's the wrong way. Stop and choose your reaction so you can monitor and manage your emotions and see how your tendencies impact others around you. My favorite self-coaching question is, "How are you teaching others to relate with you?"

MAINTAINING CLEAN BOUNDARIES

Healthy boundaries are where you can freely and safely define yourself without blurring into others or being intruded upon by them. Assertiveness is essentially keeping and protecting your boundaries; know what's your responsibility and what's theirs. "Not my circus. Not my monkeys." Just as you have to protect your physical space, you also have to protect your emotional space.

Unhealthy boundaries can manifest in oversharing, inappropriately disclosing personal problems, nagging, the inability to say no to others' demands, allowing people to take advantage of or criticize inappropriately, smothering, excessive meddling, and over-gifting.

Other examples of poor boundaries are wanting inappropriate socializing with colleagues, the need to solve everyone's problems, and dishing out unsolicited advice.

The telltale signs of poor boundaries in coaching leadership involve projection and ego. When you project as a leader, you try to manage and lead team members the way you like to be managed or led if you were in their position. Or you assume you understand them and superimpose what you think is best for them, telling them what to do and how to do it. This communicates to them that you are right and they're less right. This breeds dependency in passive employees and resentment in competent ones. Poor leadership boundaries can also cause you to treat your team as an extension of your ego. If they figure out your ego is riding on the success of the team, they will smell your desperation and ego fragility. This makes the team's success or failure about you. Would you want to be led by a desperate egomaniac?

If your boundaries are loose, it can show up as a need to be liked, which may lead you to befriend your team inappropriately or to get your social needs met by the team. The need to be liked or that "disease to please" is deep-seated for some. Whether you figure out how that need can be met outside of work or you simply learn how to put it aside at work, it's essential that you don't allow it to color the way you lead. If you do, you'll be at the mercy of other people's moods and reactions, where you allow others to dictate how you think, feel, and behave. Most of all, your leadership will become about you and your fragile ego.

If you're an over-sharer, be careful of this loose boundary. Some self-disclosure is appropriate, but too much information or sharing of your personal issues or stories can blur the lines for both you and others. Remember, you are colleagues, not best friends. You are their leader, not their peer.

If your boundaries are too rigid, it can show up as the need to be right. You may feel compelled to advise or point out others' mistakes in order to meet your own need for significance or sense of competence. This can shame and demotivate people, and you'll lose their trust and respect. Meet your needs for competence, significance, and growth elsewhere, not when you are trying to help others to meet theirs and lead them.

As a leader, you have more leeway to impinge on other people's space because you have more power. For instance, you may assign more responsibility to a team member who always says yes. Your job as a leader is to help them to tidy their boundaries to avoid being railroaded or taken for granted, especially by you. If you're impinging on their social or emotional space, they may not feel they're in a position to tell you to back off. Not only is it a manifestation of poor boundaries, but it can go so far as to feel like abuse.

What do you do if other people on your team have poor boundaries? Protect your boundaries by learning when and how to say no and when to walk away from someone who is socially and emotionally intrusive. For example, if they give you unsolicited advice, take up too much of your time, or use emotional currency to manipulate you ("This is all so complicated. And it's just that you're the *only* one who understands me."), respond assertively to delineate and clarify boundaries. Try saying, "I want to discuss this with you, but I won't be able to do it justice right now. How about we meet up tomorrow a few minutes before work or over a quick lunch?" Remember, you are teaching others how to respect your time and boundaries and you are modelling to your team members how to employ assertiveness in their own interactions.

DISCLAIMER

Just because we have research supporting self-awareness and its correlation with effective leadership, it does not give us permission to become self-absorbed or self-important. I've seen too many self-development junkies who become so focused on their own self-esteem and personal development that self-care becomes a boundless self-love affair. The worst is when they equate self-understanding with understanding others: "Since I know what it's like for me, I know what it's like for you." See how easily that can be flipped around to feign empathy: "I know what it's like for you because I know what it's like for me in that situation." The danger lies in focusing on how you see your own reflection in others in this narcissistic trap.

Trade secret in keeping clean boundaries: *Repeat this mantra, "This is not about me."*

CHAPTER 3 KEY POINTS

- Clean boundaries provide space and clarity to distinguish between what's your issue and what's not. Know where you end and where the other person begins.
- Self-awareness is a fundamental key to keeping clean boundaries.
- Identifying your core values, learning to recognize your own imperfections and biases, and knowing your own emotional temperature are all helpful tools for developing your self-awareness.

CHAPTER 4

Focus and Listen

How can focused listening
improve your communication?

Some people define communication as "it's not what you say, but how you say it." I find that idea too simplistic. Applauding elegantly with one hand does not produce clapping. Recognize that the "co" in communication indicates that it's a joint venture in which we have reciprocity. So, let's rephrase: "Communication is what you say, how you say it, and the response you get."

In order to welcome a response, we leave space open for the other person to talk and for you to be quiet and focus on what they're saying. We have been told it's important to actively listen. However, what they don't tell you is that you may find yourself becoming overactive listeners. Your mind will buzz with your own "stuff"—thoughts, ideas, advice, expectations, biases, judgments, and jokes—that will prevent you from staying focused on the other person and what they're saying.

This chapter identifies the most common mistakes we make that keep us from being quiet, neutral, and present listeners and dives into what real attentive listening looks like.

MECHANICS OF LISTENING

On average, we can listen to and process 125 to 250 words per minute. However, we think more quickly than that, around 1,000 to 3,000 words per minute. This means we are easily distracted by our own thoughts when we think we're listening.

After listening to someone, we can recall only 20 percent to 50 percent of the content after an hour and remember even less if we dislike the subject or the speaker. As human beings, we are very subjective and selective about what we focus on, which can make us poor listeners if we're not interested or entertained. And generally, we like to believe what we say is more interesting than what others are saying. All this is worrying, considering that about 50 percent to 85 percent of what we learn is through listening.

All the experts talk about active or responsive listening in communication training. Once you hear the words *active* and *responsive*, what do you picture in your head? Too many people misconstrue them as enthusiastic and responding type of listening. In fact, I'm surprised poor listening isn't a sporting category, considering how so many people are competing for airtime, jockeying for position, running their mouths, jumping to conclusions, throwing in their two cents, wrestling with ideas, running interference, and sparring to prove their point! No wonder there are so many social injuries considering how active and strenuous listening can be.

People often take active to mean *overactive* or *reactive*. They take in information while simultaneously thinking about what to say next or debating between responding with reason (the head) or feeling (the heart). But if you're so busy with what YOU are thinking, feeling, and doing, you're not focusing on the other person, are you?

Many people stop listening when they assume they understand. Because the brain takes the path of least resistance, it takes shortcuts and jumps to assimilate the incoming information with what it already knows. Then your brain tells your mouth to say things that are relevant to your familiar narrative rather than staying focused on the other person's unique story and experience.

For example, your office mate tells you her laptop got infected with a virus last night and she lost her presentation notes for the pitch she's leading this morning. This evokes a vivid memory of your I-thought-I-was-going-to-die moment when you realized you brought the wrong thumb drive of your PowerPoint slides when you arrived at a conference last year. Your brain releases this memory-driven adrenaline and your mouth feels compelled to share your story. So yes, you can sympathize with your office mate, but you can't stop thinking, "Oh, that reminds me of what happened to me!" Whatever your colleague says, you'll listen through your own filter rather than being able to tend to her and her thunderous moment. It takes effort to steer away from that impulse and practice focused (on the other person) listening, which removes you from the equation and leaves complete airtime to the other person.

FOCUSED LISTENING

Focused listening means being intentionally present for the other person without judgment, bias, or assumptions. So again, remember clean boundaries here: You listen with focus. They talk. You ask attentive and moving questions. They talk out the answers. You ask more moving questions. They tease more things out. The conversation is focused on their narratives and answers. Here is an exchange with a client:

> **Coach:** What's on your mind today?
> **Manager:** I finally got promoted to manage the global team. My biggest fear is becoming a micromanager.
> **Coach:** Congrats on the promotion! Hmmm. A micromanager. So tell me, generally how do you like to be led or managed?
> **Manager:** Give me an outline of the goals and let me loose. I go away, figure stuff out, and then I deliver. And I always deliver. Probably why I'm getting promoted.
> **Coach:** How did you figure out you prefer to be independent?
> **Manager:** I didn't like my bosses hovering or telling me what to do. I don't need all that hand-holding.
> **Coach:** So, micromanagement is what you fear because your independence and freedom are important to you?

Manager: Yeah, of course.

Coach: For those who are not as independent or confident, and who don't want or need that freedom, what do you think their management fears are?

There was no need for me to hijack the conversation with leadership stories or project what I might assume he is thinking/feeling or advise him on how he can transition to this promotion. I could have thought, "What could I say that would impress this client?" But this was not about me and what I know. It was about honing in on what he knows and listening to focus on what his needs were. He wanted to be a good manager and get things right.

In this case, I was able to use him as the instrument to answer his own questions. I didn't need to bore into his fears and analyze them. What he needed was for me to bear witness to his potential fear of being what he thinks is a bad manager. We then bypass this fear by removing himself from the equation; we don't focus on him or his fears. We redirect him to look at what his team may need or fear.

GETTING HOOKED

The previous section was all about boundaries, which define where you end and the other person begins. Here, we'll apply that principle to conversations. Too often in conversation, you find yourself reacting emotionally as soon as the other person says something that pushes your buttons. Your visceral reaction is what I describe as being "hooked." You know you've been hooked when emotion flares inside of you, and your strongest desire is to jump in there. When someone really annoys you, it says more about *you* and less about the other person's behavior.

I worked with a client who was struggling with why his team was seeking mentorship from other leaders in the organization. He wondered why they would go to another manager for support when they had him as their manager. When he found out his direct report was going through a horrific divorce and missing work due to depression, my client was upset and complained why she had not come to him: "I can't believe she didn't tell me what was going on. I'm her supervisor. Imagine how embarrassed I was when my managing director asked how she was doing, and I didn't know what he was talking about. I know how awful divorce is. I've been divorced twice. I know what she's going through." Rather than focusing on his direct report, my client was more upset and embarrassed about being left out of the loop.

I reflected that he seemed disappointed about her inability to trust him. I also asked what he thought about her depression and missing work. We discussed which part of this situation was about him and which was about her. What did she need, and what did he need? What was really important? He admitted he was annoyed that she didn't trust him, and he took that as a criticism. (You'll notice it's still about him.) We discussed ways in which he could be more engaged with his team overall so he could be more approachable.

Once my client's buttons were pushed, he had lost his power to be there for the other person. Focused listening is about taking the focus off yourself and shifting it onto the other person.

This is why self-awareness is a prerequisite to boundaries, and boundaries are a prerequisite to being a good listener. Keeping your focus on the other person results in good listening, which goes hand in hand with understanding. When you're up to date on your own personal "intel," you're less likely to get hooked and lose the ability to be present for the other person. You retain your own footing when you separate your issues from the other person's. If you care too much or judge too much, you can easily get hooked.

Trade secret to listening: Be the neutral and curious observer of the drama.

CHAPTER 4 KEY POINTS

- Communication is what you say, how you say it, and the response you get.
- Focused listening means being intentionally present for the other person without judgment, bias, or assumptions.
- Avoid "getting hooked" and letting your own emotions or visceral reactions get in the way of you listening.

CHAPTER 5

DO EMPATHY

∞∞∞∞∞∞∞∞∞∞∞∞∞∞∞∞∞∞∞∞∞∞∞∞∞

How can adopting a new approach to empathy
help you enhance your coaching leadership skills?

∞∞∞∞∞∞∞∞∞∞∞∞∞∞∞∞∞∞∞∞∞∞∞∞∞

E mpathy is a highly valued skill in our society. Studies
show most employees believe empathy is one of the most
important traits for leaders. Patients respond better to empathic
doctors and students to empathic teachers. We often blame the
lack of it as the root of our relationship, communication, and
leadership problems.

But what *is* empathy, really? While for some people understanding
and wielding empathy comes as naturally as breathing, for others
it's not so easy. And, given its complexity and humanity's still
loose grasp on the matter, it's no wonder.

The concept of empathy was coined in the early 1900s by
American and British psychologists and thinkers, who took the

term from the Greek word *empatheia,* meaning passion. At the time, the word described the state of projecting one's feelings onto the other person or onto the world. A similar definition from that era is understanding the world the way you see or feel it.

In the theory of art appreciation, empathy refers to how appreciation depends on the viewer's ability to project their personality into the viewed object. The German word *einfurlhung,* or "in-feeling," describes how one would "go into" a piece of art to experience what the artist was feeling.

By the mid-1900s, the definition of empathy had expanded, becoming more multilayered and closer to how we now understand it in the context of emotional intelligence: the capacity to know or imagine another's thoughts or feelings, adopting the posture of another, feeling as another does.

If this all sounds vague and projective, that's because it is. Despite empathy being a recent business concept and practice, social scientists have been studying it for over a century and there is still no clear-cut definition. One thing that neuroscientists have concluded is that our brains are wired to mirror others (and they go so far as to imply we are naturally geared for empathy at some level). Still, how did empathy go from Greek passion to psychological and artistic projection to emotionally understanding other people?

To clarify the confusion a bit, neuroscientists and psychologists have distinguished two types of empathy: emotional and cognitive. Needless to say, they don't include passion or dangers of projection as the original scholars and philosophers did.

Emotional empathy is the ability to mirror and *feel* what the other person is feeling or experiencing and to respond with appropriate emotion to that person's state. This may also be described as emotional contagion or mirroring. Not everyone can or wants to do this at work. Then there are people who do too much of it.

Cognitive empathy is the capacity to take the other person's perspective by interpreting or supposing what it could be like for the other person. This requires imagining or pretending. This is akin to walking in someone else's shoes and also called perspective taking. (We will discuss the questionable hygiene of wearing someone else's shoes later.)

Researchers make it clear that this capacity does not mean you understand the other's experience as they experience it, but you might feel their feelings the way *you* understand them using your own range of experience. This harkens back to the original definition of empathy from the early thinkers. Regardless of whether the meaning is old or new, emotional or cognitive, the end goal of empathy is for the other person to feel and to think they are understood, and this can't happen unless they feel and think they are heard and seen.

How do we even know or measure how much someone is heard, seen, or understood?

Let go of worrying about whether you're *feeling* empathy or imagining yourself being somebody else. Other people feel or think they're being heard when you are present, focused, and listening to them. This is doing empathy.

Doing empathy starts with accepting that the other person is different from you. Their circus, their monkeys. The next step is to be present and to listen to them as if they're teaching and you're learning.

You are not distracting yourself to assume their feelings or putting yourself in their position. I know this goes against the ancient adage of walking a mile in someone else's shoes or putting yourself in someone else's shoes. Literally and emotionally, wearing someone else's footwear is unhygienic. It's like a commercial pilot without any military training that says she knows how a fighter pilot feels during combat. Will she really empathize by flying that jet for a thousand miles?

You may not understand and sometimes honestly don't care about the sequence of events or the details of what happened to them, but when you make the time and effort to be present and listen, *you are demonstrating you care that they care about what happened to them, and that's <u>doing</u> empathy.*

Shared experience does not equate to automatic empathy, emotional or cognitive. You can relate to it or it can resonate with you, but you can't assume that their world and view are the same as yours. Research on differing eyewitness reports of the same incident by multiple people show how everyone experiences the same event in their individual way. You may understand other people's pain but not the specific struggles that make each person's pain unique.

In doing empathy, avoid assumptive, judgmental, or leading statements:

I know exactly what you mean.
This must be so hard for you.
I've been there, I know what you're going through.
You must be devastated.
It's not that bad, at least…
If I were in your position, I would…
I understand how you feel.

Consider the following statements to convey you are present and they're being heard:

I can't begin to imagine, but that sounds difficult.
I think I can relate to some of that.
I can only begin to imagine what that's like.
Oh, I didn't realize that.
I can appreciate where you're coming from.
I wouldn't think to do that, but I can see why you did.
That's never happened to me, and I could only guess how hard that could be for you.
Wow…I don't know what to say.
I've had a similar thing happen to me, but everyone experiences these things differently.
I'm sorry that's happened to you.
That sounds like a bummer.
I hear what you're saying.
I'm sorry this is happening to you.
I'm sad to hear that.
How did you respond to that?
What was it like for you?
How are you managing?
What can I do to help?

Doing empathy is safer, simpler, and much quicker than feeling empathy or pretending you're the other person. It's a form of clean boundaries. It can also be a relief to those whose personalities are more logical, rational, or cerebral. Doing empathy in a nutshell: *You may not have to care about or fully understand what's happening to the other person, but you have to care that they care about what's happening to them.*

EMPATHY TRAPS

Too Much Empathy

Countless books, coaching workshops, seminars, training programs, and conferences on empathy send a clear message: Empathy is a total good, an indispensable tool for understanding, leading, and empowering others. But can there be too much of a good thing? Highly emotionally empathic people are the ones who cry along with their friend who just lost their dog. They're also the people screaming out loud in the movie theatre when the babysitter's attacker jumps out from the dark. They feel or vividly imagine what it's like to experience what others are experiencing.

This is not the type of empathy we need in leaders. Those very high on the empathy spectrum run the risk of overidentifying with someone else's experience so strongly that their own intense experience can get in the way of objectivity or reason, making them less effective. Doctors don't have to feel a patient's devastation when they deliver the difficult news about a diagnosis. While it is certainly helpful for them to be sensitive and considerate in that moment, more importantly we need them to maintain emotional equilibrium so that they can effectively do their job of treating us. Those who are high on the feeling empathy spectrum may need to create more professional distance and be acutely aware of their own emotional cues.

Shared Experience

Empathic response is, to some degree, limited by the range of your own experience and possibly embellished by your imagination. The fact of the matter is that it's impossible to *exactly* know what someone else is experiencing. Many assume that shared experience means shared understanding. That is true only to an extent. Be aware everyone is unique and the rule for shared experience and empathy is that you may understand them generally, but not specifically. For example, let's look at two different people getting promoted at work. One person feels accomplished, flattered, excited, and is already planning a celebratory vacation with the extra money that will accompany the new job title. They assume the other person feels just as elated and celebratory. The other person? They generally feel the same sense of accomplishment, prestige, and flattery but are filled with sheer dread that the job title and more money mean more responsibilities, weekends lost to chasing deadlines, and time away from their family.

Another shared experience is being in lockdown during the COVID-19 pandemic. A global crisis causes the generally shared experience of shock, fear, and coping, but the specifics of how we struggle to cope are unique from person to person. In short, you understand another person's pain but not necessarily their struggle. This is why you don't generalize or assume your empathy, but you ask and listen to personalize that empathy one person at a time.

Watch out for the pitfalls of pseudo-empathy of, "I've been there. Done that. Got the T-shirt!" and "Same thing happened to me, so I know exactly how you feel!"

Projection

Projection is when we use feelings, thoughts, and reactions from our own experience as a lens to assume we understand others' feelings, thoughts, and reactions. Projection leads us to presuppose we already know what the other person is talking about, which invariably stops us from really listening.

Related to projection is when we use our existing knowledge to fill in gaps in stories to try to understand. The most basic illustration of this is when you read, "twinkle, twinkle…" you're already assuming and humming, "…little star." We tend to do this with other people's stories. This is more about your attempt to predict, not to understand. There are even people who want to join you in your story that they finish your sentences! This is a form of hijacking because they're more interested in predicting and synchronizing with your words; they're not really listening to your content.

Prejudice

Prejudice can also hinder effective empathy. Studies show that we tend to empathize more easily with people who resemble ourselves. Social psychology and jury studies show we exhibit a greater inclination to sympathize, empathize, and feel compassion towards people who are similar to us in race, gender, religion, level of attractiveness, values, or class. This is part of your self-insight test: In what ways might you be treating your clients, colleagues, or employees differently depending on how closely you identify with them or how closely they resemble you? Recognizing differences in how you see and treat others can help you be more aware, which helps to manage yourself and others. See if you can practice empathy equally with different people you encounter.

You hear on the news that there was a hurricane that ripped through your old hometown, devastating the people in it. Even though you no longer live there and don't know anyone there now, your interest in the news about the town is far greater than the hurricane in a town you've never heard of or visited. Prejudice also applies to confirmation biases and halo effects. Your prejudgment or bias is an empathy trap because you assume you understand, and when you assume, you stop listening and learning.

Trade secret to empathy: Empathy is not assuming you understand, it's ensuring the other person understands their own story/problem/issues. Also, **you may not care about or fully understand what's happening to them, but you do have to care that they care about what's happening to them.**

CHAPTER 5 KEY POINTS

- There are two types of empathy—emotional and cognitive—and whether or not empathy comes naturally to you, anyone can "do" empathy.
- Be aware of empathy traps, like exercising too much empathy, projecting, or prejudging.
- Walking in someone else's shoes can be unhygienic.
- You may understand other people's pain but not the specific struggles that make each person's pain unique.

CHAPTER 6

ASK MOVING QUESTIONS

<><><><><><><><><><><><><><><><><><><><><><>

What are moving questions and how can they
develop people and ideas?

<><><><><><><><><><><><><><><><><><><><><><>

*"If I had an hour to solve a problem and my life depended on the
solution, I would spend the first 55 minutes determining the proper
questions to ask, for once I know the proper questions, I could solve
the problem in less than 5 minutes."* —Albert Einstein

Curiosity is one of the traits of great leadership. The biggest
value of asking questions is not about getting the answers
but to help others think more creatively and with possibilities.
Questions help them to understand. Questions empower.

Your curiosity is a clear expression of your interest and attention.
When you ask curious questions in response to what the other

person is saying, it's proof that you're present, interested, and listening. It shows your desire to understand and learn. Asking the right question at the right time can change someone's life.

The art of conversation at work straddles the fine balance between being social and professional. An exceptional leader is socially professional in meetings and professionally social at office parties. At social gatherings, you hear people talking over each other. Those who talk the loudest and fastest win. If you're the leader, this shouldn't be you. Your rank or title is loud enough. Lead with questions to draw others out, not by hogging the limelight.

WHY VS. WHAT AND HOW

There are six kinds of questions you can ask: when, where, who, what, why, and how. The first four are information questions. When? Now. Where? There. Who? They. What? This and that. You'll get the facts. They are all important questions and have their place and time. My favorite questions, however, are *why* and *how,* which are narrative questions that give you the story and a way into someone's thoughts and feelings. Okay, I have to confess, I also have a soft spot for *what.* When we use *what* to expand possibilities, it becomes an enabling question.

Why questions can be intellectually seductive, because once you have figured out why someone did something, you feel like you've solved a mystery. Very satisfying. It can give the impression of clarity. If you're interested in knowing the motive, intention, or cause behind something, then the *why* question is useful and compelling.

However, *why* questions can lead to guessing, theorizing, and navel-gazing. Answers to *why* questions may be reactive without resolution. You can easily tumble down the rabbit hole of conjecture and blame, which means you, as the inquirer, don't have as much control over the dialogue. *Why* questions tend to fix you in the past, and memories can be quite subjective.

What questions tend to keep you in the present, and *how* questions favor the future. Using *what* and *how* questions proactively keeps you and the other person in fact-focused and action-oriented space. I have a motto for developing confidence: "Do something, anything, just one thing toward your goal." That one thing will lead to two, then three, and so on. Such incremental progress builds confidence. I follow up with moving questions:

> What needs to happen to get things going?
> What's one thing you are able to do today?
> How do you want to take this first step?
> How could you generate enough energy to lead yourself to the next thing?
> How do you want to move forward from here?
> What do you think about that?

As a brief aside, if the most useful word in coaching leadership is *how*, the second-most useful is *else*. They think they've listed all options. You ask, "What else can you do?" or "So what else would help you?" or "How else could you look at this?" or "Who else do you know that could help you?" *Else* has a way of pushing the limit and can help someone imagine a way to get unstuck and moving with one word. Half the time, you might either get silence or "I don't know." It's important you stay with that silence and with the discomfort of not knowing.

Returning to the value of *why* and *how* questions, here are two scenarios in which someone is responding to a friend worried about a job interview.

Scenario 1

>**Friend:** I think I bombed that interview.
>**You:** No, you didn't. Why do you think that?
>**Friend:** I don't know.
>**You:** I'm sure it went fine.
>**Friend:** I'm really nervous to find out.
>**You:** Why are you nervous? You have nothing to be nervous about. You did your best.
>**Friend:** I just don't think I got what they're looking for.
>**You:** Why don't you think more positively?

Scenario 2

>**Friend:** I think I bombed that interview.
>**You:** What happened at the interview?
>**Friend:** I was so nervous and I really screwed up on one of the questions.
>**You:** One question? How many questions did they ask?
>**Friend:** Tons, it was a long interview….
>**You:** One out of tons of questions. What do you think about that?
>**Friend:** Yeah, I guess I'm fixated on that one question. But I don't think I'm what they're looking for.
>**You:** How do you know for sure?
>**Friend:** I guess I don't.
>**You:** How do you want to keep yourself busy until you find out for sure?

Friend: Apply for more jobs and do more mock interviews.

Which scenario do you think was more effective, and what patterns did you notice about using *why* versus *what* and *how* questions? Scenario 1 denies your friend's feelings, which can be dismissive. If someone is afraid, they have the right to feel afraid. Disagreeing with them or telling them to think more positively won't help. Questioning why they feel that way or telling them to stop feeling that way certainly doesn't work either. If it were that easy, the slogan "Just Say No" should have abolished our global drugs problem decades ago.

PITFALLS

Cautions on "Why" Questions

Let's take a closer look at some of the common pitfalls that accompany *why* questions.

They can feel like criticism. A danger of asking a *why* question is that it assumes a motive for a behavior and can imply criticism or blame, which might shut some people down. A *why* question also implies cause and effect, which may lead us to reach for a convenient explanation. Any way you put it, there's a danger in promoting linear thinking instead of comprehensive thinking. If you're interested in clarifying the picture, instead of asking, "Why did you do that?" and placing focus on motive, try asking, "How did that happen?" or "What happened?" This works beautifully with children at home and with adults at work.

They focus on the past rather than the present. Another danger of a *why* question is that it focuses more on the past and less on the event or experience itself. You may be giving the message you're more interested in what came before the incident and less about the situation at hand. This can lead to overanalyzing, and that leads to analysis-paralysis. You go in circles fixated on why things happened when you could be using the energy to figure out how you can move forward. As you move forward proactively, the *why* either becomes less important or it will become obvious.

Their interpretation depends on power dynamics. *Why* questions can also sound judgmental or challenging depending on the power dynamics between the people in the conversation. If an architectural apprentice asks a staff architect, "Why are the beams a different weight in those two rooms?" it conveys curiosity. If someone senior to the staff architect asks the same question, the architect may scramble for a defense. A better question would be, "How did you decide on the beams in those two rooms?" The question may sound the same but reframing it as a *how* question facilitates dialogue rather than demands answers, puts the architect less in a defensive position, and ultimately is more conducive to receiving suggestions for change. Instead of questioning or challenging, a *how* question says, "Walk me through what or how it happened; I'm interested in how you got there" or "I'm listening; tell me more."

Unsolicited Advice in Disguise

We have a funny way of asking, "Why don't you...?" as a question, when we're really trying to give sneaky unsolicited advice. Remember: Unsolicited advice is usually not welcome. When you start any suggestion with, "Why don't you...?" it generally sounds patronizing, as though you are assuming the other person isn't bright enough to have thought of the solution.

Also, be careful of the phrases "If I were you…" and "If you were smart…." Statements that start this way are glib. After all, how likely is it that the advisor has deeply considered what they would do if they were in your situation? This advice is all about them. They don't really care about what you could do; it's what *they* would do. Meanwhile, "If you were smart…" is just an insulting way of suggesting anything to anyone.

"How Does That Make You Feel?"

One of my biggest pet peeves about seeing therapists depicted on TV or in movies is when the client says something meaningful and the shrink invariably asks, "So how does that make you feel?" When I see this used in other coaching training, I'm aghast. I'll let you in on a psychological secret: There's a subconscious jab embedded in that question. Once you see what's beneath the surface of that question, you'll think twice about using it in your conversations.

> **Client:** The boss decided to send Curtis to the Singapore meeting to present our project instead of me.
> **Coach:** What happened?
> **Client:** Apparently, I'm "needed" here to initiate the new project.
> **Coach:** How does that make you feel?
> **Client:** Crappy.

On the surface, the question sounds harmless, but it gives the illusion that the situation makes him feel crappy. We're in the business of empowering people, and the question carries a disempowering jab because it implies something "out there" dictated his feelings. Use the question cautiously. "How do you feel about it?" is actually a healthier question than "How does that make you feel?"

If you want to empower and motivate your team or clients, help them to recognize and own their reactions. No one controls them unless they give up the power to do so. No one programs them and *makes* them feel or think a certain way. We don't have control over how others behave or how a situation unfolds, but we get to choose how we respond to them.

"I Don't Know."

Just as there is no such thing as a stupid question, there is no such thing as a stupid answer. Even the simplest answer is always a good place to start. Heck, even if there's no answer, I see that as a great opportunity to ask moving questions. The most dreaded answer, though, is "I don't know." Some say that's not an answer. I say it's not only a good answer, it's also a vulnerable self-disclosure. It tells me that someone doesn't trust what they're thinking or doesn't trust what I will do with what they're thinking. Or they simply don't know.

Whatever the reason, what do you do with that response? Never take "I don't know" as the final answer. Doing so is admitting you're stuck, and worse than that, you're letting them off the hook. Try the following questions to move forward from the "I don't know":

Which part don't you know?
If you don't know, what would you like to know?
What would you need to find out?
What would help you to know?
Let's pretend you did know. What would you say?
If you were to take a wild guess, what would your answer be?

And here's my favorite deep but shrink-y query, "What's it like for you not to know?" You use this when both of you have trust and are ready to delve in to process their insecurities and confidence issues.

Moving Questions: How and What

Moving questions are fact based and forward thinking. They keep you grounded in the present and keep you actioning towards the solution and the future. Simply, they keep you moving forward.

Here are some easy alternative and empowering questions that will engender ownership of feelings, thoughts, and reactions:

What was that like for you?
How did you respond to that?
How was that for you?
How did you feel about that?
What mixed emotions come up for you?
If you're speaking with someone who doesn't access their feelings readily, start with these. Some people need to process their cognitive responses first before they can start processing how they feel, and vice versa.
And your reaction was…? (Pause, so they can fill in.)

What went through your mind when you heard that?
What was it like to see that happen?
What was your reaction when _____? (Fill in the blank.)
What did you think about that at the time?
What do you think about that now?
How did you make sense of that?
How would you like to make sense of that?

Closed-Ended vs. Open-Ended

There are three basic types of questions: closed-ended, open-ended, and rhetorical. There's a loose 80/20 rule when it comes to asking questions in coaching leadership: 80 percent are open-ended and 20 percent are closed-ended.

Closed-ended questions require a simple, definitive answer. These are quick transactions where the questions are based on who, what, when, and where. You are asking if something is or is not and are not going beyond gathering information or clarifying.

Open-ended questions are about stories and possibilities. They are questions that invite the respondent to be thoughtful, creative, innovative, analytical, or imaginative.

Rhetorical questions are posed to make a point without really expecting or wanting an answer. Generally, you'll ask a rhetorical question to drive home a point or to be dramatic or sarcastic. Avoid these!

Closed-ended questions can be useful if you want the bare facts and a quick confirmation or check-in. They're useful when you need quick data on the status of things. These questions are often posed to elicit a yes-or-no answer, but to be fair, they're a bit wider reaching than that. Possible answers to closed-ended questions can be anything from "yes" or "no" to "not yet," "maybe," "I don't remember," or "I don't know."

Here are a few examples of useful closed-ended questions:

> Can you fix it?
> Is the team ready for _____?
> Did you finish the presentation?
> When will you get it done?
> When are we meeting?
> Were you surprised?
> Who was there?
> Is there a bonus with this deal?
> Did you like the package?

Close-ended questions are also useful when you want to establish a starting point or set the stage for follow-up or probing questions.

> Are you happy with the offer?
>> No.
>>> What can we do to make this deal more enticing for you?

> Were you happy with the service?
>> Yes.
>>> How would you feel about leaving feedback for us online?

Warning: As a coaching leader, beware of the fact that closed-ended questions can kill a conversation in its tracks, especially if the person you are addressing is not very verbal or doesn't trust or like you. Some managers are famous for these killers:

> Didn't you get my memo?
> Do you think the tone was right? (Alternative: How did the edits change the tone?)
> Are you okay with the changes I made? (Alternative: What did you think about the changes?)
> Do you have anything to add? (Alternative: What else could make this more compelling?)
> Did others have any complaints or comments? (Alternative: How could we get some more feedback?)

Closed-ended questions can also squelch creativity in others:

> Can you think of something to add here?
> Could you make that look better?
> Would you do the same again given the chance?
> Did you exhaust all options?
> Did you see anything you can change?

You may also opt to ask a closed-ended question if you're asking just to ask. We do this all the time, to the point where a narrative answer to "How are you?" surprises us.

"Was it a good meeting?" This is not only a closed-ended question but is also a leading one, because you leave the qualitative expectation in the air. What if the meeting was bad? You haven't left space for them to tell you that the meeting was anything other than good, and the prospect of sharing that may bring about worry of bringing the mood down or disappointing you. Stuck for what to ask? Here are some open-ended, productive questions to pull out of your hat.

Purpose-Rendered

These help to affirm motivation:

> What's the endgame?
> What purpose does this serve for you?
> Which values does this tick for you?
> What's most useful for you?
> What fires you up about this?
> How does this bring meaning to the work you do?
> In what way is that important for you?
> What's most important for you? How come?
> What fans your fire? How will you sustain that burn?

Solution-Focused

These are handy when you want to hammer out solutions with someone. Be prepared to bite your tongue—your advice trigger will be itching! Stay calm and ask:

> What have you tried so far?
> What worked and what didn't?
> What would you rather have?
> What would you like to do instead?
> How else could you approach this?
> What else can be done?
> What other ways could you look at this?
> What's needed here to get a better perspective?

How do you want it to look?

What is your desired outcome?

What would success look like?

What will that do for you?

What results do you want?

What timescale are we looking at?

What's a manageable deadline?

How do you want to track your progress?

What problems are you exchanging here?

Action-Oriented

These are not for the faint of heart. No navel-gazing allowed here.

What will kick you into gear and get you motivated?

What's your first step? What's the next one? And the next? What else needs to happen?

What and when is your final step?

How much will it hurt if this doesn't get done? How much will it cost?

What will you lose if this doesn't happen? What will you gain if this happens?

What's the collateral damage? Can you live with that?

How badly do you really want this?

If you get this, what are you giving up?

What are the negative consequences of getting this?

If you say no to this, what are you saying yes to?

If you say yes to this, what are you saying no to?

What would happen if you did nothing?

If you couldn't use _____ as a reason/excuse, how would you move forward?

Creative

These work really well with artistic and expressive people.

> What would you rather be?
> How would you rather feel?
> How do you want to feel?
> What would you like to see happen?
> How do you see yourself? Where are you as you're doing this?
> Where would you like to take it, and how far?
> How can you turn that problem into a means to your goal?
> What will it look, sound, or feel like when you have achieved this goal?
> What if...?
> What are other ways this could work?
> What else might be true?

Big Picture

These questions take a step back for perspective.

> What are the various consequences of doing that?
> What assumptions are you making?
> If you look back five years from now, what advice would that older you give the present you?
> What seems irrational? What do you think/feel about that irrationality?

Trade secret to moving questions: Keep your focus on what they need, not what you need.

CHAPTER 6 KEY POINTS

- When you're not sure, you ask.
- Asking moving questions harnesses the power of curiosity to help your team members perform at their best.
- Common pitfalls to asking moving questions include asking misguided why questions, giving unsolicited advice, asking how that makes someone feel, and failing to make the most of "I don't know" responses.
- Moving questions can be: closed-ended and open-ended (depending on what the situation requires), purpose-rendered, solution-focused, action-oriented, creative, and big picture.

CHAPTER 7

Do Immediacy

~~~~~~

How can you be ready to respond in the moment?

~~~~~~

You know that feeling when you're put on the spot, cornered, surprised, insulted, offended, stuck, or speechless? And you wished you had been ready with a quick, eloquent reply to alleviate the tension? Do you feel relieved when someone says, in an awkward moment, "Man, we could cut this tension with a knife!" *Immediacy* is a tool you can use to break, reset, or redirect tension. It distracts from pressure, breaks the ice, and buys emotional time to help you get your bearings. It's also the most useful tool to pull out when you make a faux pas. A simple "Oops, my bad" will do the trick.

Immediacy is a behavioral mirror you put up to see what's happening right now. It's a powerful intervention taught in team therapy training to break tension. The practice involves calling out the facts of the action in the room without judgment, which invites people to pause and get a common perspective. Besides allowing a pause in what might be a fraught moment, the practice can reveal what everyone is doing, thinking, or feeling. This moment of self-awareness sometimes helps stop a difficult situation from spiraling out of control.

I use immediacy a lot in my team coaching with executives, teaching them to understand how they come across to other people. By noting their immediate experience, they learn how they impact others and how they react to others. I might say, for example:

> Monica, others are talking over you. What would you like to say to them?
> Greg, what did you mean when you said Monica is passive?
> Lee, how do you think others see you when you're this vehement about your idea?
> What are you guys really arguing about here?

Practicing immediacy is also good for coaching yourself. If you're feeling overwhelmed by something, self-talk with immediacy is a way to test your hunches about what may be going on.

> "I'm taking this too personally."
> "She pushes my insecurity buttons."
> "This is not my issue. I need to let it be."
> "Not my circus. Not my monkeys."
> "She reminds me of my old boss. It's not her."
> "Is this just my thought or is it fact?"

Use immediacy when you're stuck, shocked, disappointed, offended, scared, mistaken, embarrassed, or in any other situation where you find you don't know what to say. It will relieve the immediate tension, and you will get your bearings back by reinforcing trust and reestablishing boundaries.

You can disarm most people with immediacy. My top immediacy when I'm being derided, criticized, or disrespected is a lighthearted "Oh, don't be like that...." Whether or not someone is being a jerk, it helps if they see you're not fazed.

At a Q&A after a famous pharmacology expert finished his talk at a conference, a female scientist stood up to ask a question that challenged his theory: "How can you advocate using this drug when there may be a problem with the reuptake?" With condescension, the speaker replied, "If you don't understand basic cell biology, I can't explain it to you!" The whole room went silent. Instead of sitting down embarrassed and allowing the whole room to pretend it didn't happen, she immediated, "Oh professor, don't be like that. We're just trying to have a discussion here." Instead of meeting the speaker head on, the delegate redirected his force. She could have also said, "It seems we have stunned the room to silence," or "How does your response add value to the spirit of an open discussion we're trying to have now?" or "My ignorance aside, are you deflecting the question?" or "It appears you prefer not to address my question publicly."

Remember to ask such questions with a genuine tone of curiosity. If not, you'll be in danger of sounding sarcastic. Like most things in communication and conflict, when you take yourself or your ego out of the equation, you have more purchase and control.

Be the observer and the participant simultaneously so there are three in a room: you, the other person, and the "observer" of the dynamics between the two. We also call it "observing the drama."

OBSERVE AND SUMMARIZE

You observe and state what you are observing without assuming it as fact. By summarizing what you're seeing, you are teaching others that you are assertive without being confrontational. It's an invitation, not a criticism.

> Oh, that was my mistake.
> This is really awkward.
> Our conversation is getting too heated to be constructive.
> This silence is killing me.
> It's hard when we argue like this.
> We're at a standstill.
> I think we're at that "agree to disagree" place.
> There's been a miscommunication.
> That came out all wrong.
> We're going in circles.
> I just interrupted you, didn't I?

Avoid starting your observation with "you," because in a sensitive situation that "you" will seem like a pointing finger. Once someone becomes defensive and feels cornered, constructive conversation will shut down.

CLARIFY

Check to see if you're understanding something as it was meant to be conveyed. Ascertain whether everyone is on the same page. Clarification is done with questions.

There are three clarifying questions that work in any awkward situation or when you're stuck:

> What do you mean by that?
> How does this help you? Us?
> How is that adding value to our situation?

When asked with genuine curiosity, these questions are not sarcastic or critical. They simply put the onus on the other person to explain while buying time to prevent you from emotionally reacting.

I once used this when a man inadvertently said something sexist at a team meeting. Everyone heard, it was awkward, and everyone hoped he hadn't said it. I could have let it go, but that would teach him that it's okay to say such things. I could have been offended, taken it personally, and put myself in the equation. I could have told him exactly what I thought of him. That would have meant I had been emotionally hooked, and that could have escalated the situation. Instead, I curiously and gingerly asked him, "Bob? What did you mean by that?" This stumped him. He had to respond to my genuine curiosity. I also asked him how his message (not he) may have come across. We discussed his traditional and religious views and how he was raised to think a certain way about women and men. He didn't apologize, nor was I asking him to. Will his views get in the way of working with certain clients and colleagues? Yes. Does he want to change? No. Did the team understand the norm about being free to be different? Yes. Will I take on awkward conversations? Yes.

Other useful clarifying questions:

> How do you think I understood that?
> How did we get here?
> What are we really arguing about?
> Is this awkward for everyone else, or is it just me?
> Did that idea just get dropped like a lead balloon?
> When you're upset like this, what can I do?
> Could we push the "reset" button?
> Could we start this over?
> What's the endgame here?
> Did you really mean to say _____?
> Did I offend you?
> Did that sound like BS to you as it did to me? Let me try again.

SHARE

This is probably the hardest immediacy tactic because you have to provide feedback or self-disclose. However, it's powerful because it's a way to own the communication without putting another on the defensive. This is where appropriate humor or self-deprecation comes in handy. Use "I" to own it. Use "this" or "that" to make it less personal.

OMG, my bad!

I'm such a jerk for saying that.

That came out all wrong. Could I try again?

Did I just say that out loud?

When our conversation gets heated like this, I lose my motivation to continue.

I think I've just been offended.

This is really hard for me.

I don't know how to respond when you raise your voice like this.

I didn't realize how hard it was going to be to discuss this.

I feel you're disrespecting my ideas when you interrupt me like that.

I'm not clear about my own reaction to that. I'm going to let that sink in a bit.

If that's how you understand it, I don't know what to say.

I feel patronized when you speak to me like that.

Oh, don't be like that.

I feel really left out when you two argue like this. (Using humor to break up a fight.)

Trade secret to doing immediacy: Trust & obey your gut feelings. Be braver.

CHAPTER 7 KEY POINTS

- When in doubt, do immediacy.
- Immediacy is the practice of addressing something in the moment and is a tool you can use to break, reset, or redirect tension.
- Ways to do immediacy include being neutral and braver, observing and summarizing without judgment, clarifying with questions, and sharing through feedback or self-disclosure.

CLOSING COMMENTS

I hope this book serves as an accessible and useful toolkit for anyone who leads and coaches a team. The five principles of coaching leadership—cleaning your boundaries, focused listening, doing empathy, asking moving questions, and doing immediacy—have been distilled from hundreds of professional and personal development books and relationship research, and from thousands of hours I have spent training, teaching, counseling, and coaching clients. If you walk away from this collection of practical and rational principles with only one thing, may it be this final message: Take yourself out of the equation. Leading, coaching, and understanding someone else happens *through* you; it's not *about* you.

Acknowledgments

Special thanks to my best friend and life's sister, Carolyn Gee, who has supported me in all ways imaginable for the last 35 years. The wind beneath my wings. I wouldn't have made it this far without you. You have held my hand through this book, page by page, line by line.

Big shout out to my amazing mentors and life's parents, Thomas Parham, Gene Awakuni, and Seymour Bryson, who believed in me, lifted me up, and sheltered me through many storms. Colonel Bill DeMarco, thank you for that kick in the right direction. Massive thanks to my friends and beta readers, who also happen to be gifted editors: Karen Eng, Emily Chenette, and Matthew Day. I want to reach out to the MBA students and alums at the Cambridge Judge Business School; thanks for keeping me young and on my toes. And to Morgan Gist MacDonald at Paper Raven Books, thank you for your patience and cheerleading and for the drinks in Paris. Great appreciation to the PRB team for editorially and operationally making this book happen. And Karen, thank you for the GSD!

REFERENCES

Aurelius, Marcus. 2019. *Meditations*. SDE Classics.

Bradberry, Travis. 2009. *Self-Awareness: The Hidden Driver of Success and Satisfaction*. New York: Putnam.

Bradberry, Travis and Greaves, Jean. 2009. Emotional Intelligence 2.0. TalentSmart.

Branson, Richard. 2014. *The Virgin Way: How to Listen, Learn, Laugh and Lead*. London: Virgin Books.

Brown, Brené. 2010. *The Gifts of Imperfection: Let Go of Who You Think You're Supposed to Be and Embrace Who You Are*. Center City, MN: Hazelden.

———. 2018. *Dare to Lead: Brave Work. Tough Conversations. Whole Hearts*. New York: Random House.

Carnegie, Dale. 1936. *How to Win Friends & Influence People*. New York: Simon and Schuster.

———. 2010. *How to Stop Worrying and Start Living*. New York: Simon and Schuster.

Collins, Jim. 2001. *Good to Great: Why Some Companies Make the Leap and Others Don't*. New York: Harper Business.

Dweck, Carol. 2017. *Mindset: Changing the Way You Think to Fulfil Your Potential*. London: Robinson.

Cherniss, Cary and Mitchel Adler. 2000. Promoting Emotional Intelligence in Organizations. Alexandria, VA: American Society for Training and Development.

Covey, Stephen. 1989. *The 7 Habits of Highly Effectively People.* New York: Simon and Schuster.

Davies, Michaela, Lazar Stankov, and Richard D. Roberts. 1998. Emotional Intelligence: In Search of an Elusive Construct. *Journal of Personality and Social Psychology,* 75(4):989–1015.

Downey, Myles. 2014. *Effective Coaching.* LID Publishing.

Eurich, Tasha. 2018. *Insight: How to Succeed by Seeing Yourself Clearly.* London: Pan Macmillan.

Feldman-Barrett, Lisa and Peter Salovey (eds). 2002. *The Wisdom in Feeling: Psychological Processes in Emotional Intelligence.* New York: Guilford Press.

Gagliardi, Gary (translator). 2014. *Sun Tzu's The Art of War.* Clearbridge Publishing.

Goleman, Daniel. 1995. *Emotional Intelligence: Why It Can Matter More Than IQ.* New York: Bantam Books.

Isaacson, Walter. 2015. *Steve Jobs.* New York: Simon and Schuster.

Jeffrey, Scott. 2017. Core Values List. https://scottjeffrey.com/core-values-list/

Lencioni, Patrick. 2002. *The Five Dysfunctions of a Team: A Leadership Fable.* San Francisco: Jossey-Bass.

Leuner, B. 1966. "Emotional Intelligence and Emancipation." *Praxis der Kinderpsychologie und Kinderpsychiatrie.* 15:193–203.

Mayer, John D., Peter Salovey, and David R. Caruso. 2002. Mayer-Salovey-Caruso Emotional Intelligence Test (MSCEIT): User's Manual. Toronto, Ontario: Multi-Health Systems, Inc.

McKee, Annie. June 5, 2015. "Quiz Yourself: Do You Lead with Emotional Intelligence?" *Harvard Business Review.* https://hbr.org/2015/06/quiz-yourself-do-you-lead-with-emotional-intelligence.

McLaren, Karla. 2013. *The Art of Empathy: A Complete Guide to Life's Most Essential Skill.* Louisville, CO: Sounds True.

Perel, Esther. 2020. *How's Work?.* Podcast. Gimlet Media. Via Spotify.

Peters, Steve. 2013. *The Chimp Paradox: The Mind Management Program to Help You Achieve Success, Confidence, and Happiness.* New York: TarcherPerigee.

Salovey, Peter and John D. Mayer. 1989. "Emotional Intelligence." *Imagination, Cognition and Personality,* 9(3):185–211.

Salovey, Peter, Marc A. Brackett, and John D. Mayer. 2004. *Emotional Intelligence: Key Readings on the Mayer and Salovey Model.* Naples, FL: NPR, Inc./Dude Publishing.

Sandberg, Sheryl. 2013. *Lean In: Women, Work, and the Will to Lead.* New York: Knopf.

Scott, Kim. 2019. *Radical Candor: Be a Kick-Ass Boss without Losing Your Humanity.* New York: St. Martin's Press.

Sinek, Simon. 2017. *Leaders Eat Last. Why Some Teams Pull Together and Others Don't.* London: Portfolio.

Stibitz, Sara. Jan 30, 2015. "How to Really Listen to Your Employees." *Harvard Business Review.* https://hbr.org/2015/01/how-to-really-listen-to-your-employees.

Su, Amy Jen. 2019. *The Leader You Want to Be: Five Essential Principles for Bringing Out Your Best Self—Every Day.* Brighton, MA: HRB Press.

Sugar, Alan. 2010. *What You See Is What You Get: My Autobiography.* New York: Macmillan.

Tuckman, Bruce W. and Mary Ann C. Jensen. 1977. "Stages of Small-Group Development Revisited." *Group & Organization Management*, 2(4),419–427.

University of Toronto. June 2, 2000. "Discovery Shows How Brain 'Fills In Blanks' To Help Us See." ScienceDaily. www.sciencedaily.com/releases/2000/06/000601164617.htm.

Wiens, Kandi and Darin Rowell. Dec 2018. "How to Embrace Change Using Emotional Intelligence." *Harvard Business Review.* https://hbr.org/2018/12/how-to-embrace-change-using-emotional-intelligence.

Winfrey, Oprah. Feb 5, 2011. "A Transformational Leader." Video. https://www.youtube.com/watch?v=9zDMoj7D3b8.

———. Apr 28, 2014. "Oprah Winfrey on Career, Life, and Leadership." Stanford Graduate School of Business. Video. https://www.youtube.com/watch?v=6DlrqeWrczs.

———. 2014. *What I Know for Sure*. New York: Flatiron Books.

Yalom, Irvin D. 2005. *Theory and Practice of Group Psychotherapy*. New York: Basic Books.

———. 2019. *Becoming Myself*. New York: Basic Books.

Zahariades, Damon. 2017. *The Joy of Imperfection: A Stress-Free Guide to Silencing Your Inner Critic, Conquering Perfectionism, and Becoming the Best Version of Yourself*. Independent publication.

Ziglar, Zig. 2019. *Goals: How to Get the Most Out of Your Life*. Cumberland County, PA: Sound Wisdom.

Printed in Great Britain
by Amazon

38828486R00069